young exceptional children

chil____en

Monograph Series No. 16

Blending Practices for
All Children

ISSN: 1096-2506   978-0-9905128-0-6

Disclaimer

The opinions and information contained in the articles in this monograph are those of the authors of the respective articles and not necessarily those of the editors of the Young Exceptional Children (YEC) monograph Series or the Division for Early Childhood (DEC) of the Council for Exceptional Children. Accordingly, DEC assumes no liability or risk that may be incurred as a consequence, directly or indirectly, or the use and application of any of the contents of this monograph.

DEC does not perform due diligence on advertisers, exhibitors, or their products or services and cannot endorse or guarantee that their offerings are suitable and accurate.

Published and Distributed by:

Division for Early Childhood
3415 S. Sepulveda Blvd.
Suite 1100, Unit 1127
Los Angeles, CA 90034
Phone: 310-428-7209
Email: dec@dec-sped.org
Website: http://www.dec-sped.org

The Division for Early Childhood (DEC), a division of the Council for Exceptional Children, is an international membership organization for individuals who work with or on behalf of young children with disabilities and other special needs. Founded in 1973, DEC's mission is to promote policies and advance evidence-based practices that support families and enhance the optimal development of young children who have or are at risk for developmental delays and disabilities. Information about membership and other resources available can be found in www.dec-sped.org.

Suggested citation:

Pretti-Frontczak, K., Grisham-Brown, J., & Sullivan, L. (Eds.) (2014). *Blending practices for all children* (Young Exceptional Children Monograph Series No. 16). Los Angeles: Division for Early Childhood of the Council for Exceptional Children.

A Message From the Editors

Combining beliefs, values, traditions, and practices to best serve all young children

Welcome to the sixteenth volume of the Young Exceptional Children Monograph Series. In this volume we focus on the growing visibility of quality services for children from birth through age eight. Increased attention to early care and education provides opportunities to advocate for equal access, participation, and success for all young children. The ideals of meeting the needs of all children are grounded in a rich tradition and set of values that describe "inclusion." And while inclusion as a philosophy or value statement was once a topic of much debate, it is now an expected practice measured through federal and state accountability and performance standards. The journey from beliefs to practice has been bumpy, rough, and at times, met with reluctance.

We propose the idea of "blending" as a logical evolution of practices. We hope for a more rapid journey to blended practices than occurred with the adoption of inclusion, meaning that our hope is that blending soon becomes the rule, rather than the exception. As a start toward this goal, we offer Monograph #16 as a collective effort to propel the evolution and application of practical approaches and services for all young children.

As we capitalize upon the idea of *blending* as the primary theme of YEC's Monograph #16, it is important to examine the context in which the term originated, and how blending is currently conceptualized. The editors of Monograph #16 conceptualize blending as the act of combining beliefs, values, traditions, practices and even funds from multiple disciplines, sources, and perspectives to maximize our efforts in serving all young children.

Efforts to illustrate a blended approach have been depicted in what has been termed the *curriculum framework*. Beginning in early 2000, a collaborative writing project culminated in setting the foundation that resulted in elucidation of the basic premises and elements of a curriculum framework (DEC 2007). Over time, we've refined how the curriculum framework "smooths" the boundaries between philosophies, approaches, and practices, culminating in a fully articulated approach to serving children with diverse abilities (Grisham-Brown & Pretti-Frontczak, 2013).

Specifically, we have described the curriculum framework to include four blended elements, including assessment, scope and sequence, activities and instruction, and progress monitoring (see Grisham-Brown, Hemmeter, & Pretti-Frontczak, 2005; Grisham-Brown & Pretti-Frontczak,

2011; Grisham-Brown & Pretti-Frontczak, 2013). Each of these elements is blended in the sense that teams are encouraged to:

- Gather, document, and summarize information about groups and individual children using a wide variety of techniques from pedagogical documentation, which ranges from Reggio Emilia inspired practices to functional behavioral assessments stemming from applied behavior analysis
- Recognize the developmental and learning trajectories that depict the interrelatedness of development, and recognize that all children have needs that can be viewed as tiered or varied (i.e., at any particular time a child may exhibit strengths, may struggle, and may have intensive needs)
- Cull from the research, the recommended practices, and professional wisdom that has evolved for intervening and teaching both children with and without identified disabilities and delays
- Analyze and interpret different databases when answering questions about children's performance in attaining universal or common outcomes, targeted outcomes with which they are struggling, and individual developmental outcomes that undermine their access, participation, and progress

In addition to the four elements of blended practice, we've come to recognize that blended approaches require a number of supporting practices to ensure full implementation and efficacy. These supporting practices include a strong leadership team, a commitment to data driven decision-making, the formation of collaborative partnerships, and ongoing and sustained professional development. The relevant work of Grisham-Brown and colleagues further describes these critical supports.

In our opinion, blending "smooths" the implied forced choices among colleagues, policies, and paradigms, and expects the creation of flexible environments, characterized by data-driven choices for intervening, thoughtfully considered by teams serving young children and their families.

Overall, when we think about blended practices, we presume the following ideals:

- Blending requires purpose and can't be accomplished ad hoc or incidentally
- Blending requires intentional inquiry and decision-making
- Blending is based on relationships among providers and can't be achieved in silos
- Blending requires commitment, time, preparation, and ongoing support

In an effort to continue to articulate what blended practices may look like in early childhood, we challenged the contributing authors to translate their work into reader-friendly articles, which will inform and transform the field's knowledge of blending. We also asked them to share what blending means to them as a way to understand how their article informs our conversations about blended practices. Here is what they had to say:

- Campbell and Milbourne: "Using different types of teaching practices together – in other words blending instructional practices that are delivered to children (or groups of children) explicitly so that a particular skill will be learned over time with environmental practices intended to enhance and support child/children's immediate participation in daily activities and routines."
- Dorsey, Danner, and Laumann: "Creating a high-quality early childhood environment that blends developmentally appropriate practices with DEC recommended practices."
- Dinnebeil and McInerney: "A blending of evidence-based practices that describe an intentional model of intervention (itinerant ECSE services) that will support successful inclusion of young children with special needs in community-based early childhood programs."
- Barton, Bishop, and Snyder: "Blending intentional teaching with embedded instruction includes setting the occasion for children's learning and ensuring sufficient opportunities to respond."
- Grisham-Brown, Pretti-Frontczak, Bachman, Gannon, and Mitchell: "Successfully implement instructional strategies, originally designed for teaching children with disabilities, with children with a variety needs so they may learn individualized outcomes."
- Catlett, Maude, Nollsch, and Simon: "Offering examples of how to blend the best of the early childhood field and the early childhood special education/early intervention field by using strategies that produce knowledgeable, reflective, and collaborative professionals."
- Kennedy and Lees: "Practices which enhance opportunity and full participation in inclusive settings by aligning developmentally appropriate practices and family/community-sensitive strategies, all toward the goal of optimizing the development of infants and toddlers with special needs."

We thank the authors for their efforts to meet our challenge and to help move the field forward with the blending of practices. Building upon the authors' work, we offer a final resource at the end of the Monograph. In the "Moving Forward" section, we include select resources highlighted in the Monograph. The selected resources are ones the editors believe can be used to further assist readers' efforts to implement blended practices.

For each resource, a suggestion is provided for how to use or apply the content to practice as a teacher/provider, administrator, technical assistance provider, or faculty member. Our hope is that this set of select resources will provide readers with additional ideas for how to implement or support others to implement high quality programs that *work* for ALL young children.

References

Division for Early Childhood [DEC] (2007). *Promoting positive outcomes for children with disabilities: Recommendations for curriculum, assessment, and program evaluation*. Missoula, MT: Author.

Grisham-Brown, J., & Pretti-Frontczak, K. (2013). A curriculum framework for supporting young children served in blended programs. In V. Buysse and E. Peisner-Feinberg (Eds). *Handbook of response to intervention (RtI) in early childhood*. Baltimore: Paul H. Brookes Publishing Co.

Grisham-Brown, J., & Pretti-Frontczak, K. (Eds.). (2011). *Assessing young children in inclusive settings. The blended practices approach*. Baltimore: Paul Brookes Publishing Company.

Grisham Brown, J., Hemmeter, M.L., & Pretti-Frontczak, K. (2005). *Blended practices for teaching young children in inclusive settings*. Baltimore: Paul H. Brookes Publishing Co.

Co-Editors   Kristie Pretti-Frontczac, Ph.D.
Jennifer Grisham-Brown, Ed.D.
Lynn Sullivan, M.Ed.

Frameworks for Response to Intervention in Early Childhood:

Description and Implications

The Division for Early Childhood of the Council for
Exceptional Children (DEC)
27 Fort Missoula Road Suite 2
Missoula, MT 59804 www.dec-sped.org

National Association for the Education of Young Children
(NAEYC)
1313 L Street, NW Suite 500
Washington, DC 20005-4101 www.naeyc.org

National Head Start Association (NHSA)
1651 Prince Street
Alexandria, VA 22314 www.nhsa.org

Purpose This paper, "Frameworks for Response to Intervention in Early
Childhood: Description and Implications," has been jointly developed by
the Division for Early Childhood of the Council for Exceptional Children,
the National Association for the Education of Young Children, and the
National Head Start Association. The purpose of the joint paper is to
define early childhood response-to-intervention frameworks and to promote a broader understanding and discussion of the topic.

Across the nation, there is an increased focus on ensuring that all young
children experience positive outcomes and enter school ready to learn.
Moreover, significant national investments have been made to align policies and resources to support the implementation of research-based
teaching and caregiving practices within all programs and classrooms,
from early childhood to postsecondary settings. One key piece of legislation that underscores the increased attention and investment in intervening early is the reauthorization of the Individuals with Disabilities
Education Improvement Act of 2004 (IDEIA 2004).

IDEIA includes a specific provision highlighting the need for early intervening services (EIS) for K–12 students (with a particular emphasis on children in K–3) who require additional academic and/or behavioral support. This provision aims to reduce or eliminate the future need for special education. Early intervening services ensure that students who are not currently identified as needing special education or related services, but who need additional instruction or intervention to succeed in a general education environment, receive the necessary support in an appropriate and timely manner. The EIS provision was added in order to align IDEIA with the goals and accountability measures that were a part of the 2001 reauthorization of the Elementary and Secondary Education Act (ESEA), which is much more commonly known as No Child Left Behind (NCLB 2002). In fact, the IDEIA statute and commentary reference the ESEA 162 times. Early intervening services generally have been organized under frameworks known as *response to intervention* (RTI) or *multi-tiered systems of support* (MTSS) (National Early Childhood Technical Assistance Center [NECTAC] 2012; Walker & Shinn 2010). These and other shifts in policy and practice provide important opportunities for early childhood practitioners to work closely together to support the development and learning of all young children. As RTI has become an important part of how educational programs are organized within schools serving children in kindergarten through 12th grade, there has been increased interest in the application of RTI to young children (NECTAC 2012).

The Division for Early Childhood (DEC), the National Association for the Education of Young Children (NAEYC), and the National Head Start Association (NHSA) have created this joint paper to provide guidance on the relationship of RTI frameworks to the unique contexts of early childhood (EC) programs.[1] The collaborative paper has three purposes: first, to present a broad definition and description of the features of RTI frameworks as they are evolving in EC; second, to provide a description of common misconceptions about RTI in EC; and third, to identify future directions related to RTI research and practice in EC. It is, however, beyond the scope of this paper to offer specific examples regarding implementation strategies, to provide full descriptions about the pros and cons of RTI approaches, or to discuss different interpretations of RTI features. The paper is designed to help those working in EC conceptualize the common features of RTI frameworks, to understand why there are dif-

[1] While the term *early childhood* generally refers to a period from birth to grade three, the issues associated with RTI have, to a large degree, been defined for students in K–3, while the practices for infants, toddlers, and preschoolers are still evolving. Therefore, this paper addresses RTI frameworks as they may apply to young children from birth until entry into school-age programs. The application of the features discussed here, however, may apply to K–3 settings as further refinement of RTI approaches for students are made.

ferences across states and programs, and to stimulate further discussion about the application and utility of RTI in EC.

While states and local programs have conceptualized RTI for young children in many different ways, the focus of this paper is on the common features of RTI frameworks in EC, how they are designed to ensure high-quality teaching and responsive caregiving for all young children. Readers should note, however, that the science or practice of RTI for young children is still evolving, and this paper is based on current conceptualizations and practices.

Context for RTI in K–12 and Early Childhood Education

Although current federal statute does not specifically mention the use of RTI, IDEIA broadly describes the applicability of such frameworks as part of EIS, and Section 681 states that the US Secretary of Education will develop a comprehensive plan for Subpart 2 of the Act following input from relevant experts. Further, NCLB promotes the use of schoolwide reforms that ensure children have access to scientifically based instructional strategies, and frameworks such as RTI are clearly aligned to this mission. In fact, as Congress prepares to reauthorize ESEA, special education organizations such as the Council for Exceptional Children (CEC 2010), the Council of Administrators of Special Education (CASE 2011), and others have issued recommendations calling on Congress to include provisions that would require a proportion of ESEA funds to be used for early intervening services, and to include language that provides guidance regarding the use of RTI.

That said, while key principles of RTI approaches are a component of federal statutes (e.g., NCLB 2002; IDEIA 2004), these principles have always been the focus of high-quality intentional teaching and caregiving efforts in EC. Among the core principles of various RTI approaches that align with recommended practice in EC are the following:

- specification of a multi-tiered system of supports;
- early provision of support or intentional teaching/caregiving with sufficient intensity to promote positive outcomes and prevent later problems;
- use of child data to inform teaching and responsive caregiving practices; and
- use of research-based, scientifically validated practices to the maximum extent possible (Batsche et al. 2005).

Again, such principles are at the core of EC recommended practices related to assessment, intentional teaching, differentiated instruction, and ongoing progress monitoring (Copple & Bredekamp 2009; Division for Early Childhood, 2007; NAEYC & NAECS/SDE, 2003; Sandall et al. 2005).

While tracing the historical and contemporary context of RTI as applied in K–12 (see Fuchs et al. 2003; Batsche et al. 2005; Graner, Faggella-Luby, & Fritschman 2005; Hollenbeck 2007; Jimerson, Burns, & VanDerHeyden 2007; National Center on Response to Intervention 2010) is beyond the scope of the paper, it is important to understand that RTI approaches have evolved as a response to two primary concerns:

1. An existing "wait to fail" model in which teams had to wait until a child/student demonstrated a significant discrepancy between intellectual ability and academic achievement (that is, failed) before determining that he or she had a learning disability and thus was eligible for special education services.
2. A commonly occurring practice in which students were identified as having a delay or disability without consideration of the quality, type, or relevance of teaching efforts they may have received in general education settings prior to this identification.

These two concerns fueled changes to federal regulations, state rules, and district policies and led to the widespread implementation of a variety of RTI approaches (Berkeley et al. 2009). Demonstrations of the effectiveness of RTI in K–12 settings (e.g., Gersten, Chard et al. 2008; Gersten, Compton et al. 2008b; Gersten et al. 2009; Torgesen 2009; Glover & Vaughn 2010; Shapiro et al. 2011) have led to discussions about potential applications in EC (e.g., VanDerHeyden & Snyder 2006; VanDerHeyden et al. 2008; Fox et al. 2010; Buysse, Peisner-Feinbert, & Burchinal 2012). Until recently, RTI has been viewed as a K–12 initiative, but many programs and states are applying RTI in EC programs because the core principles align with EC recommended practices (Greenwood et al. 2011).

Understanding the context for RTI in K–12 may be useful for helping to inform implementation of RTI in EC; however, as the authors cited above and others have noted, adoption of frameworks and practices used with older children are often not be appropriate for younger children. Programs for young children (birth until entry into school-age programs) are under the direction of a variety of agencies (for example, education, health and human services, child care), resulting in services provided in diverse settings including public school classrooms, family child care homes, community child care centers, and Early Head Start and Head Start programs. Personnel with highly variable preparation and training (no formal education in early childhood, child development associate degree, early childhood certification, master's degree, teacher's license and other licenses) are responsible for teaching and responsive caregiving in these programs. Moreover, the resources available for implementing RTI frameworks vary across early childhood programs. Additionally, the developmental needs of young children addressed in early education and care settings are broader than those addressed in K–12 schools. Thus, the context and subsequent application of RTI approaches within EC are sufficiently different from those in K–12 and warrant discussion and exploration by the fields of early education, intervention, and child care.

Definition and Features of RTI Frameworks in Early Childhood

Here we provide a general definition of RTI in the EC context and then outline features found in RTI frameworks in EC.

Defining RTI in EC

Response to Intervention in EC may be seen as a means of providing high-quality teaching and responsive caregiving through the delivery of differentiated support for all young children. In other words, in EC, RTI frameworks are a means for implementing a hierarchy of support that is differentiated through a data-based decision-making process (Greenwood et al. 2011; National Professional Development Center on Inclusion 2012).

Figure 1, "Illustration of an ECE RTI Framework", presents one way of conceptualizing an ECE RTI framework. Specifically, the triangle represents three tiers of teaching and/or caregiving. Tier 1 represents high-quality teaching and responsive caregiving that should be available to all young children. Tier 1 is purposely depicted as wider than Tiers 2 and 3 to symbolize its function as the foundation for other practices. And it is proportionally deeper than Tiers 2 and 3 to indicate that more intensive support or instruction are less likely to be necessary if high-quality Tier 1 support and instruction are in place. Similarly, Tier 2 is depicted as proportionally deeper than Tier 3 to indicate that the added implementation of effective Tier 2 support and instruction reduces the need for highly individualized Tier 3 efforts. The arrow going up (and down) the left side of the triangle illustrates that teaching and responsive caregiving efforts increase (or decrease) in intensity and frequency, and individualization is more (or less) specialized as a child's needs in a particular area increase (or decrease). The up and down arrows in the center of the triangle indicate that RTI frameworks should be dynamic in nature. The cycle around the triangle in Figure 1 further illustrates the iterative

Figure 1.
Illustration of an ECE RTI framework.

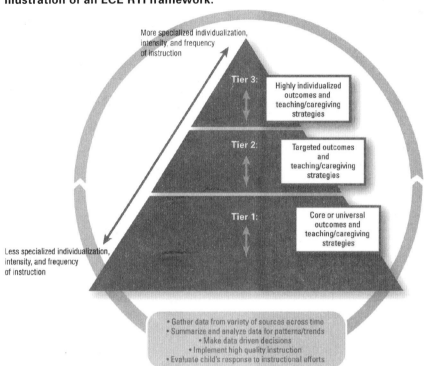

More specialized individualization, intensity and frequency of instruction

Tier 3:
Highly individualized outcomes and teaching/caregiving strategies

Tier 2:
Targeted outcomes and teaching/caregiving strategies

Tier 1:
Core or universal outcomes and teaching/caregiving strategies

Less specialized individualization, intensity, and frequency of instruction

• Gather data from variety of sources across time
• Summarize and analyze data for patterns/trends
• Make data driven decisions
• Implement high quality instruction
• Evaluate child's response to instructional efforts

and dynamic process of gathering, summarizing and analyzing, decision making, implementing, and evaluating. Iterative processes are often used in RTI to implement systems of support or instruction and to evaluate responses to teaching and caregiving practices.

Through such dynamic and iterative processes, teams revise or change any number of variables including **what** is taught, **where** the child is taught, **when** the child is taught, and **how** the child is taught. The goal of implementing an RTI framework with young children is to be aware of areas (academic, behavioral, etc.) in which each child has differing needs and to match instructional and behavioral systems of support to those individual needs. Creating a match between teaching/caregiving and children's needs requires a means for implementing a hierarchy of support that is differentiated through a data-based decision-making process.

Features of Early Childhood RTI Frameworks

As RTI frameworks have evolved in EC, four common features have emerged: multi-tiered systems of teaching and caregiving practices; a high-quality curriculum; ongoing assessment and continuous progress monitoring; and collaborative problem solving among team members.

Multi-tiered systems of teaching and caregiving practices. These systems are based as much as possible on research-validated approaches (Sugai & Horner 2009). Teaching and caregiving practices are used within and across tiers to support the diverse needs of individual and groups of young children. The number of tiers in an RTI framework varies; however, the notion is that the bottom tier is comprised of the core or universal content as well as foundational teaching and caregiving practices deemed appropriate for all young children. The next tier (or set of tiers) usually refers to supplemental teaching and caregiving practices that are provided for children who may benefit from more support. While the nature of supplemental practices varies depending on the outcome being addressed and the age of children involved, commonly used strategies include extra scaffolding, repetition, and guided practice in the context of developmentally appropriate activities and routines. The top tier is composed of highly individualized teaching and caregiving practices. These practices are designed to support children in learning skills that are critical or considered prerequisite to achieving common outcomes being addressed at the bottom tier.

An important feature of multi-tiered systems of support is that the type and intensity of support is matched to children's needs versus placing a child at a particular tier. Matching support means a child may receive different levels of intensity or instruction/caregiving for different outcomes. For example, a child may receive Tier 1 literacy instruction while at the same time participating in Tier 2 instruction related to a social-emotional outcome. Likewise, a toddler might receive Tier 1 caregiving strategies that support his or her development of expressive language to get wants and needs met, while simultaneously obtaining Tier 3 instruction for walking without support. Again, children are not identified for a specific tier of instruction across outcome areas, and EC teams do not label a child as being a Tier 2 or Tier 3 child. Rather, a child may change in his or her need for a specific tier of instruction given the demands of the situation or the outcome identified, and thus can "move within and across tiers." If a child is receiving a higher tier of support related to a specific outcome area and progress-monitoring data demonstrate that the child is making adequate growth toward that outcome, the intensity of instructional support would be reduced or the type of instructional support provided would be changed. Similarly, if progress-monitoring data demonstrate that a child has not responded to the enhanced support, practices from a higher tier of instruction might be added. Across the tiers, teams can increase the level of support, the frequency with which planned instruction is delivered, or the degree to which outcomes are individualized (Grisham-Brown & Pretti- Frontczak, in press).

It is important to note, however, that regardless of tier or level of support, EC teams (which include family members) should adhere to recommended practices and performance standards related to effective teaching and caregiving practices (see Division for Early Childhood [DEC] 2007; Copple & Bredekamp 2009; US Department of Health and Human Services Administration for Children and Families Office of Head Start [HHS-ACF-OHS] 2011). Regardless of tier, all teaching and caregiving efforts should be planned and delivered in developmentally appropriate ways that build on children's strengths, interests, and preferences. Further, teams enhance learning and development across tiers by incorporating a variety of materials and toys within playful activities, games, and regular daily routines, and by creating interesting and engaging learning environments.

High-quality curriculum for all children. While the term curriculum has many different meanings, the term has been conceptualized as a "complex idea containing multiple components including goals, content, pedagogy, and instructional practices" (NAEYC & NAECS/SDE 2003, 6). Taba (1962) notably describes curriculum more simply as a plan for learning, while Grisham-Brown, Hemmeter, and Pretti-Frontczak (2005) define curriculum more comprehensively to include assessment for planning purposes, procedures for determining which children need what level of support, the provision of differentiation and intentional instruction, and ongoing performance monitoring. Regardless of definition, a high-quality curriculum is developmentally and culturally appropriate, is guided by team/family decisions, and employs research-based strategies that maximize differentiation and learning. Further, a high-quality curriculum within an RTI framework includes a comprehensive and relevant set of learning outcomes that serve as a guide for teaching and caregiving efforts. When working with young children, determining what is taught is primarily derived from theories of child development and associated milestones, and increasingly from state and agency early learning standards, guidelines, or foundations (Daily, Burkhauser, & Halle 2010). A high-quality curriculum at Tier 1 serves as a foundation for all other tiers of teaching and caregiving and should ensure sufficient learning opportunities embedded within daily routines and activities (Grisham- Brown, Hemmeter, & Pretti-Frontczak 2005).

Ongoing assessment and continuous progress monitoring for all children. Across RTI frameworks, terms such as *assessment,* even more widely *universal screening,* and *progress monitoring,* are used. Each term, as it applies to RTI frameworks, is described next.

Assessment is a broad term used throughout the EC literature and typically refers to a process of gathering data to make a variety of decisions, including decisions about the need to conduct further testing; a child's status compared to his or her peers; what, when, where, and how to teach; when to revise instruction; and a program's overall effectiveness (Grisham-Brown & Pretti-Frontczak 2011). Within an RTI framework, the gathering of systematic information (that is, engaging in ongoing assessment) is necessary in order to inform teaching and caregiving decisions.

Universal screening is a term used in RTI approaches and is distinct from developmental screening. Universal screening is distinct from developmental screening in at least two respects:

(1) universal screening is a process by which teams determine whether or not a child is "falling behind" and would likely benefit from additional services and/or supports, whereas developmental screening is a process by which teams to determine whether the child's development is typical and whether further testing is warranted; and (2) universal screening instruments are used to compare the child's performance to a benchmark or other criterion/standard, whereas developmental screening instruments are used to compare the child's performance to a normative sample. The systematic nature of universal screening ensures that additional or extra support is given when children need it (independent of eligibility for special education), whereas developmental screening serves as a part of child find obligations and helps teams make decisions regarding a child's need for further evaluation or monitoring.

In EC, programs can engage in the universal screening of all children's performance toward specific outcomes through the use of curriculum-based assessments or curriculum-based measures at select points across the year. For example, a home visitor may administer and interpret the results from a curriculum-based assessment (for example, *Assessment, Evaluation, and Programming System*® [Bricker et al. 2002]; *Teaching Strategies GOLD*® [Heroman et al. 2010]; or the *Hawaii Early Learning Profile*®—*HELP* [Parks 2007]) on a quarterly basis to determine if a child is responding to the family's caregiving and promotion of learning. Similarly, a preschool teacher may administer curriculum-based measures such as *myIGDIs*™ (Early Childhood Research Institute on Measuring Growth and Development, 1998) three times a year to monitor all children's performances on picture naming, sound identification, rhyming, and alliteration, which are key skill indicators of progress toward literacy outcomes.

Progress monitoring is a term used to describe the systematic and continuous process of informing decisions about whether children receiving research-based instruction or caregiving practices at any tier are responding to that instruction (Ysseldyke, Thurlow, & Christenson 1987; Raver 2003; Hojnoski & Missall 2007; Copple & Bredekamp 2009; Grisham-Brown & Pretti-Frontczak 2011; Buzhardt et al. 2012). EC teams examine trends in progress-monitoring data to see whether children's rates of learning are increasing or, alternatively, whether the children are making little or no change in their trajectories of learning. Oftentimes, progress monitoring occurs more frequently when children are receiving higher tiers of instruction. For example, progress monitoring may occur every 12 weeks at Tier 1, every 4 weeks at Tier 2, and weekly at Tier 3. Decision-making rules are typically provided to help identify when children are responding well enough to change the level of support or intensity of instruction they are receiving. For instance, a child making adequate progress for a specific length of time with Tier 3 instruction may no longer need to receive this level of individualized support and, after a prescribed period of time showing good progress, might need only Tier 2 supports to continue to make progress. On the other hand, a child receiving Tier 2 instruction might show little progress or response and, after a period of time of no growth, might require Tier 3 instruction or support. The important point here is that the system is dynamic and that children are not assigned or "stuck" in a level of support in which they show no progress. The identification of rules for determining how much change is necessary before providing children with a higher or lower tier of support is a critical aspect guiding this dynamic process.

Collaborative problem-solving process. In Response to Intervention in EC, a collaborative process helps guide teams in making decisions about quality curriculum and the use of research- based practices and supports to promote learning and in determining what an individual child needs as support for learning and development. Collaboration and partnerships between program personnel and families or other members of the community serve as the support structure for implementing RTI in EC frameworks (Al Otaiba 2005; Coleman, Buysse, & Neitzel 2006; Jackson et al. 2009). In the design of supports for individual children, those knowledgeable about the child (the teacher, family members, administrators, school psychologists, social workers) gather, document, summarize, analyze, and interpret data to see how a child is progressing and use the decision-making rules to identify which tier of support the child needs and what type of instructional strategies would help the child be most successful (Wolery 2004). These individuals collaborate to track the child's progress and determine when changes are needed.

Collaboration and establishing partnerships have long been valued in ECE with emphasis on the importance of the role of families in designing, implementing, and evaluating intervention for their children (Allen & Schwartz 2001; Christenson & Sheridan 2001; Sheridan et al. 2008). Thus, across ECE RTI frameworks, it is important for all individuals who are knowledgeable about a child to contribute to the process of determining the child's strengths, preferences, needs, and response to instructional and caregiving practices.

Misunderstandings and Misconceptions

Although there is no single or uniform way of carrying out RTI, a set of common features help define and conceptualize RTI in EC. Given the widespread movement toward implementing RTI across ages and settings, and the varied strategies used in implementation, a number of misunderstandings and misconceptions have arisen (Greenwood et al. 2011). Five common misconceptions associated with RTI in EC are discussed below.

> Misconception #1: RTI requires that children go through a multi-tiered system of supports prior to being referred to special education, thereby delaying and often restricting referral to special services.

The overarching intention of RTI is to promote positive outcomes for all children by providing timely and effective teaching and caregiving support. Through frequent data collection, those children who are not making sufficient progress receive earlier, more intensive support that is matched to their needs. The expectation is that this additional support will help improve the child's rate of learning and narrow the gap with typical rates of development. A significant assumption is that children will not have to wait for referral to special education services, including an evaluation and diagnosis, in order to obtain additional support. ***Children are not required to undergo and fail an RTI process prior to referral or evaluation for special education services*** (Musgrove 2011). Implementation of RTI frameworks in EC should not reduce or impede the rights and privileges for gaining access to special education services (Council for Exceptional Children [CEC] 2007). Further, the early intervention aspects of IDEIA clearly indicate that RTI or other related statutory language ***may not be used*** to delay appropriate evaluation of a child suspected of having a disability or delay the provision of services, and that RTI models ***may not replace*** a comprehensive evaluation (Hozella 2007). Moreover, a parent or teacher has the legal right to request an initial evaluation to determine whether a child has a delay or disability (IDEIA 2004). RTI frameworks described in this paper are intended for all children, regardless of their eligibility status or ability level.

Misconception #2: RTI focuses only on academic skills.

A fundamental element of RTI in EC frameworks is the use of appropriate teaching and care- giving practices to match the child's needs and enhance outcomes. Within RTI in EC frameworks, matched support can be appropriately applied to outcomes from any curricular area (mathematics, literacy, and science) or developmental domain (language, social-emotional, and motor), and as such does not exclusively apply to academic outcomes (Greenwood et al. 2011). To date, much of the research on RTI has focused on the areas of language and literacy (e.g., McMaster et al. 2005; Van-DerHeyden et al. 2008; Bailet et al. 2009; Koutsoftas, Harmon, & Gray 2009; Spencer et al., in press); however, there exists some research in other domains or areas of learning such as mathematics (e.g., Fuchs et al. 2005; Duhon et al. 2009) and social-emotional competence (e.g., Pearce 2009). Further, in ECE, there are multiple curricula and models for implementing supports that address a range of domains and align well with the features of RTI, including but not limited to

- Building Blocks (Sandall et al. 2002; Sandall & Schwartz 2008)
- Center for Response to Intervention in Early Childhood [CRTIEC] (www.crtiec.org)
- Curriculum Framework (Horn, Peterson, & Fox 2007; Jackson et al. 2009; Grisham-Brown & Pretti-Frontczak, in press)
- Recognition and Response (Coleman, Buysse, & Neitzel 2006; Fuchs, Buysse, & Coleman 2007; Buysse & Peisner-Feinberg 2010; Buysse, Peisner-Feinber, & Burchinal 2012;) www. recognitionandresponse.org
- Pyramid Model (Fox et al. 2003; Hemmeter, Ostrosky, & Fox 2006; Fox et al. 2010)

Misconception #3: RTI promotes teaching practices that are inappropriate for young children.

All features of RTI described in this paper align with recommended practices in EC, and the basis of any RTI framework is an emphasis on effective and differentiated teaching and caregiving practices to help all children reach intended outcomes. Concerns may arise in the implementation of RTI with young children when the practices and principles of K–12 are pushed down and applied without consideration for the uniqueness of early childhood development and learning. Concerns may also arise in the way programs choose to implement higher tiers of instruction or support within RTI in EC frameworks, because how to do so is still open to debate. EC RTI frameworks embody the characteristics of intentional teaching and developmentally appropriate practice. For example, teachers and parents can increase the level of support for children by intentionally embedding learning opportunities throughout daily routines. Teams can also provide additional support by using a wide variety of materials, creating interesting and engaging environments for purposive play and learning, and supporting prosocial behavior and peer relationships.

Misconception #4: RTI promotes the use of ability grouping, particularly in center- based programs.

At higher tiers, targeted teaching and caregiving practices might be implemented in small groups. Contrary to some perceptions about grouping, this does not imply that children are separated for all teaching or that children who need additional support are isolated from peers; such practices would be inappropriate and indefensible given the importance of peer interactions for young children. While some small-group sessions may include homogeneous groups of children, these groupings will typically occur for only a very small part of the day or for a particular activity, and participation can be optional. Small groups are a typical way of organizing learning experiences for young children in ECE programs. Targeted small group teaching is just one way of providing more intensive support, and not only homogeneous but also heterogeneous small groups may be used to provide targeted teaching. For example, a child on the autism spectrum might join in a small group of children with communication delays for a language lesson in the morning and with a heterogeneous small group of children that includes age-appropriate language models for a cooking activity in the afternoon. RTI frameworks provide opportunities for teams to provide a level of instructional intensity that a given child or small group of children need to progress, within a comprehensive and inclusive service delivery approach.

Misconception #5: The top tier of RTI is special education.

In the past, especially in K–12 models, RTI has been used as a diagnostic tool to determine if students need special education services. Appropriate use of RTI frameworks in EC includes the provision of tiers of support that consist of additional, adjusted, or more intensive teaching to meet the needs of the children being served, but is not defined by a connection to special education services. Of course, through RTI (a dynamic and fluid process), data are collected to make a variety of decisions, and the data may be useful as an aid in special-education eligibility determination. Certainly, any given child, identified or not identified for special education services, may, at some point in time, receive teaching on a select learning outcome at the foundational level of support while simultaneously receiving more intensive teaching for other learning outcomes. For example, it would be expected that children with disabilities who participate in inclusive early learning classrooms or natural environments where RTI is being implemented would be accessing and participating in the high-quality curriculum being offered to all children, while receiving more intensive supports (when needed and appropriate) on their individualized goals—but still within the context of ongoing activities and routines. While RTI in EC does not preclude identification for special education, and may support teams in making appropriate referrals for eligibility for special education services diagnoses, RTI frameworks have the goal of supporting teaching and caregiving rather than identification of a delay or disability.

The Future of RTI in Early Childhood Education

As the nation becomes more focused on the importance of the early years of development and the relationship of early experiences to future academic success, EC programs may benefit from RTI frameworks designed to ensure that each and every child receives the developmentally appropriate and intentional learning opportunities that are needed for optimal growth and learning. The implementation of RTI frameworks in EC is not without challenges, including the difficulty of applying core principles to widely diverse settings and the complexities involved with ensuring that all providers have the professional development necessary to implement the features of RTI successfully using available resources in ways that are developmentally appropriate for the children they serve. The additional demand to include related service personnel (mental health professionals, occupational and physical therapists, speech/language pathologists) in professional development efforts and RTI implementation may also pose a challenge in some settings. Other implementation challenges include

- limited research on comprehensive tiered frameworks for use with young children, particularly for infants and toddlers;
- limited research on the impact of RTI on teaching and child outcomes, particularly for infants and toddlers;
- the need for additional and adequate assessment instruments designed for the purposes described within RTI frameworks;

- the need for systems that support collaboration between general education and special education teachers, service providers, family members, and others;
- the importance of understanding how developmentally appropriate assessment, instruction, and intervention practices vary for diverse groups of children;
- blurred distinctions between the use of RTI and special education referral and delivery of services; and
- the need for greater professional development for providers on how to collect sufficient data to interpret and draw conclusions regarding children's learning and development in response to differentiated support or instruction.

All of these challenges offer directions for future research on the implementation of RTI frameworks in EC.

Opportunities through Innovation

Despite many program and system-level challenges, RTI frameworks in EC provide a number of opportunities to integrate programs and supports for all young children and their families. Unifying RTI in EC should lead to improved decision making about which supports are needed for which children and under what circumstances. Further, RTI approaches in EC offer opportunities to improve both assessment and professional development practices, and ultimately the learning trajectories of children. For example, there is growing interest in the field to use measures such as Individual Growth and Development Indicators (IGDIs) and other progress-monitoring approaches that allow ongoing assessment of an individual child's development and learning. Using such an approach allows practitioners to track a child's growth over time and guides decision making about services and supports (Slentz & Hyatt 2008; Carta et al. 2010).

The emphasis on providing research-based approaches for the provision of high-quality and responsive early education and care programs is also reflected in innovative models and approaches to professional development. The implementation of any comprehensive framework or innovation with the scale and complexity of RTI will require changes in practice. Research in professional development has resulted in a national trend across early childhood education systems to focus investments on the use of approaches that are most likely to result in supporting practitioners to implement practices likely to be effective in supporting young children's development and learning (Zaslow 2009; Zaslow et al. 2010; Snyder,

Hemmeter, & McLaughlin 2011). These approaches include (1) providing professional development that has specific and well-articulated objectives; (2) using practice-based professional development that focuses on change in practice as an outcome; (3) providing professional development activities that involve the collective participation of teachers from the same classrooms or program; (4) providing intensive activities over time rather than one-shot workshops; (5) including training on how early educators can use and examine child assessment information to evaluate the effects of their ongoing professional development; and (6) the provision of professional development that is aligned to the program's standards for practice (Sheridan et al. 2009; Zaslow et al. 2010).

Ultimately, the goal of RTI is the same as the mission that all EC teams pursue: to deliver services that help children achieve success both in school and in life. By addressing the needs of each child in a developmentally appropriate way, RTI in EC provides a critical opportunity for the field to improve outcomes for all young children.

References

Al Otaiba S. 2005. "Response to Early Literacy Iinstruction: Practical Issues for Early Cchildhood Personnel Preparation." *Journal of Early Childhood Teacher Education* 25 (3): 201–209. doi: 10.1080/1090102050250303.

Allen, K.E. & I.S. Schwartz. 2001. *The Exceptional Child: Inclusion in Early Childhood Special Education.* Albany, NY: Delmar.

Bailet, L.L., K.K., Repper, S.B. Piasta, & S.P. Murphy. 2009. "Emergent Literacy Intervention for Pre- kindergarteners At Risk for Reading Failure. *Journal of Learning Disabilities* 42 (4): 336–355.

Batsche, G., J. Elliott, J. Graden, J. Grimes, J. Kovaleski, D. Prasse, D. Tilly, et al. 2005. *Response to Intervention: Policy Considerations and Implementation.* Alexandria, VA: National Association of State Directors of Special Education.

Berkeley, S., W.N. Bender, L.G. Peaster, & L. Saunders. 2009. "Implementation of Response to Intervention: A Snapshot of Progress." *Journal of Learning Disabilities* 42 (1): 85–95.

Bricker, D., K. Pretti-Frontczak, J.O. Johnson, & E. Straka. 2002. *Assessment, Evaluation, and Programming System for Infants and Children (AEP): Second Edition Administration Guide.* Baltimore: Brookes.

Buysse, V. & E. Peisner-Feinberg. 2010. "Recognition & Response: Response to Intervention for PreK." *Young Exceptional Children* 13 (4): 2–13.

Buysse, V. E. Peisner-Feinberg, & M. Burchinal. 2012. *Recognition & Response: Developing and Evaluating a Model of RTI for Pre-K.* Poster presentation at the Fifth Annual Meeting of the Society for Research on Educational Effectiveness, in Washington, D.C., March.

Buzhardt, J., P. Walker, C.R. Greenwood, & L. Heitzman-Powell. 2012. "Using Technology to Support Progress Monitoring and Data-Based Intervention Decision Making in Early Childhood: Is There an App for That?" *Focus On Exceptional Children* 44 (8): 1–18.

Carta, J., C.R. Greenwood, D. Walker, & J. Buzhardt. 2010. *Individual Growth and Development Indicators for Young Children.* Baltimore: Brookes.

Christenson, S.L. & S.M. Sheridan. 2001. *School and Families: Creating Essential Connections for Learning.* New York: Guilford.

Coleman, M.R., V. Buysse, & J. Neitzel. 2006. *Recognition and Response: An Early Intervening System for Young Children At Risk for Learning Disabilities.* Full Report. Chapel Hill: The University of North Carolina at Chapel Hill, FPG Child Development Institute.

Copple, C. & S. Bredekamp, eds. 2009. *Developmentally Appropriate Practice in Early Childhood Programs Serving Children from Birth through Age 8.* 3rd ed. Washington, DC: NAEYC.

Council of Administrators of Special Education (CASE). 2011. *CASE ESEA Reauthorization Recommendations.* Warner Robins, GA: CASE.

Council for Exceptional Children (CEC). 2007. *Position on Response to Intervention (RTI).* Arlington, VA:CEC.

Council for Exceptional Children (CEC). 2010. *CEC's ESEA Reauthorization Recommendations.* Arlington, VA: CEC.

Daily, S., M. Burkhauser, & T. Halle. 2010. "A Review of School Readiness Practices in the States: Early Learning Guidelines and Assessments." *Early Childhood Highlights* 1 (3): 1–12.

Division for Early Childhood (DEC). 2007. *Promoting Positive Outcomes for Children with Disabilities: Recommendations for Assessment, Curriculum, and Program Evaluation.* Missoula, MT: DEC.

Duhon, G.J., E.M. Mesmer, M.E. Atkins, L.A. Greguson, & E.S. Olinger. 2009. "Quantifying Intervention Intensity: A Systematic Approach to Evaluating Student Response to Increasing Intervention Frequency." *Journal of Behavioral Education* 18 (2): 101–118. doi:10.1007/s10864-009-9086-5

Early Childhood Research Institute on Measuring Growth and Development. 1998. *Research and Development of Individual Growth and Development Indicators for Children between Birth and Age Eight.* Technical Report No. 4. Minneapolis, MN: Center for Early Education and Development, University of Minnesota. www.myigdis.com.

Fox, L., J. Carta, P.S. Strain, G. Dunlap, & M.L. Hemmeter. 2010. "Response to Intervention and the Pyramid Model." *Infants and Young Children* 23 (1): 3–13. Doi: 10.1097IYC.08073e3181c816e2.

Fox, L., G. Dunlap, M.L. Hemmeter, G.E. Joseph, & P.S. Strain. 2003. "The Teaching Pyramid: A Model for Supporting Social Competence and Preventing Challenging Behavior in Young Children." *Young Children* 58 (4): 48–52.

Fuchs, L., V. Buysse, & M.R. Coleman. 2007. *Promising Approaches to Early Intervening in the Primary Grades and Pre-K: Response to Intervention (RTI) and Recognition and Response (R & R).* Paper presented at the FPG FirstSchool Symposium, Early School Success: Equity and Access for Diverse Learners, in Chapel Hill, North Carolina, May.

Fuchs, L.S., D.L Compton, D. Fuchs, K. Paulsen, J.D. Bryant, & C.L. Hamlett. 2005. "The Prevention, Identification, and Cognitive Determinants of Math Difficulty." *Journal of Educational Psychology* 97 (3): 493–513.

Fuchs, D., D. Mock, P.L. Morgan, & C.L. Young. 2003. "Responsiveness to Intervention: Definitions, Evidence, and Implications for the Learning Disabilities Construct." *Learning Disabilities Research and Practice* 18 (3): 157–71.

Gersten, R., S. Beckmann, B. Clarke, A. Foegen, L. Marsh, J.R. Star, & B. Witzel. 2009. *Assisting Students Struggling with Mathematics: Response to Intervention (RtI) for Elementary and Middle Schools* (NCEE 2009-4060). Washington, DC: National Center for Education Evaluation and Regional Assistance, Institute of Education Sciences, US Department of Education.

Gersten, R., D.J. Chard, M. Jayanthi, S.K. Baker, P. Morphy, & J. Flojo. 2008. *Mathematics Instruction for Students with Learning Disabilities or Difficulty Learning Mathematics: A Synthesis of the Intervention Research.* Portsmouth, NH: Center for Instruction, RMC Research Corporation.

Gersten, R., D. Compton, C.M. Connor, J. Dimino, L. Santoro, S. Linan-Thompson, & W.D. Tilly. 2008. *Assisting Students Struggling with Reading: Response to Intervention and Multi-Tier Intervention for Reading in the Primary Grades. A Practice Guide.* (NCEE 2009-4045). Washington, DC: National Center for Education Evaluation and Regional Assistance, Institute of Education Sciences, US Department of Education.

Glover, T.A. & S. Vaughn. 2010. *The Promise of Response to Intervention: Evaluating Current Science and Practice.* New York: Guilford.

Graner, P., M.N. Faggella-Luby, & N.S. Fritschman. 2005. "An Overview of Responsiveness to Intervention: What Practitioners Ought to Know." *Topics in Language Disorders* 25 (2): 93–105.

Greenwood, C.R, T. Bradfield, R. Kaminski, M.W. Linas, J.J. Carta, & D. Nylander. 2011. "The Response to Intervention (RTI) Approach in Early Childhood." *Focus on Exceptional Children* 43 (9): 1–22.

Grisham-Brown, J.L., M.L. Hemmeter, & K. Pretti-Frontczak. 2005. *Blended Practices for Teaching Young Children in Inclusive Settings.* Baltimore: Brookes.

Grisham-Brown, J.L. & K. Pretti-Frontczak. In press. "A Curriculum Framework for Supporting Young Children Served in Blended Programs." In *Handbook for Response to Intervention (RtI) in Early Childhood,* eds. V. Buysse and E. Peisner-Feinberg. Baltimore: Brookes.

Grisham-Brown, J.L., & K. Pretti-Frontczak, eds. 2011. *Assessing Young Children in Inclusive Settings: The Blended Practices Approach.* Baltimore: Brookes.

Hemmeter, M.L., M. Ostrosky, & L. Fox. 2006. "Social and Emotional Foundations for Early Learning: A Conceptual Model for Intervention." *School Psychology Review* 35 (4): 583–601.

Heroman, C., D. Burts, K. Berke, & T. Bickart. 2010. *Teaching Strategies GOLD™ Objectives for Development & Learning.* Washington, DC: Teaching Strategies.

Hojnoski, R.L. & K.N. Missall. 2007. "Monitoring Preschoolers' Language and Early Literacy Growth and Development." *Young Exceptional Children* 10: 17–27.

Hollenbeck, A.F. 2007. "From IDEA to Implementation: A Discussion of Foundational and Future Responsiveness-to-Intervention Research." *Learning Disabilities Research and Practice* 22 (2): 137–46.

Horn, E., C. Peterson, & L. Fox, eds. 2007. *Young Exceptional Children.* No. 9 of monograph series Linking Curriculum to Child and Family Outcomes. Missoula, MT: Division for Early Childhood.

Hozella, P. 2007. "Early Intervening Services and Response to Intervention (Module 6)." *Building the Legacy: IDEA 2004 Training Curriculum.* Washington, DC: National Dissemination Center for Children with Disabilities. www.nichcy.org/laws/idea/legacy/module6.

Individuals with Disabilities Education Improvement Act of 2004. Pub. L. No.108-446 § 300.115 2004.

Jackson, S., K. Pretti-Frontczak, S. Harjusola-Webb, J. Grisham-Brown, & J. Romani. 2009. "Response to Intervention: Implications for Early Childhood Professionals." *Language, Speech & Hearing Services in Schools* 40 (4): 424–34.

Jimerson, S.R., M.K. Burns, & A.M. VanDerHeyden, eds. 2007. *Handbook of Response to Intervention: The Science and Practice of Assessment and Intervention.* New York: Springer.

Koutsoftas, A.D., M.T. Harmon, & S. Gray. 2009. "The Effect of Tier 2 Intervention for Phonemic Awareness in a Response-to-Intervention Model in Low-Income Preschool Classrooms." *Language, Speech, and Hearing Services in Schools* 40: 116–30.

McMaster, K.L., D. Fuchs, L.S. Fuchs, & D.L. Compton. 2005. "Responding to Nonresponders: An Experimental Field Trial of Identification and Intervention Methods." *Exceptional Children* 71: 445–63.

Musgrove, M. 2011. *Memorandum: A Response to Intervention (RTI) Process Cannot Be Used to Delay-Deny an Evaluation for Eligibility under the Individuals with Disabilities Education Act (IDEA).* www.ldanatl.org/news/osep-01211-rtimemo.pdf.

NAEYC & National Association of Early Childhood Specialists in State Departments of Education (NAECS/SDE). 2003. *Early Childhood Curriculum, Assessment, and Program Evaluation: Building an Effective, Accountable System in Programs for Children Birth Through Age 8.* www.naeyc.org/about/positions/cape.asp.

National Center on Response to Intervention. 2010. *Essential Components of RTI—A Closer Look at Response to Intervention.* Washington, DC: Office of Special Education Programs, National Center on Response to Intervention, US Department of Education.

National Early Childhood Technical Assistance Center (NECTAC). 2012. Response to Intervention in Early Childhood Resource page. http://nectac.org/topics/RTI/RTI.asp

National Professional Development Center on Inclusion. 2012. *Response to Intervention (RTI) in Early Childhood: Building Consensus on the Defining Features.* Chapel Hill: The University of North Carolina, FPG Child Development Institute.

No Child Left Behind (NCLB) Act of 2001, Pub. L. No. 107-110, § 115, Stat. 1425. 2002.

Parks, S. 2007. *Hawaii Early Learning Profile (HELP) Strands (0–3).* Palo Alto, CA: VORT Corporation.

Pearce, L.R. 2009. "Helping Children with Emotional Difficulties: A Response to Intervention Investigation." *Rural Educator* 30 (2): 34–46.

Raver, S. 2003. "Keeping Track: Using Routine-Based Instruction and Monitoring." *Young Exceptional Children* 6 (3): 12–20.

Sandall, S.R., M.L. Hemmeter, B.J. Smith, & M.E. McLean. 2005. *DEC Recommended Practices: A Comprehensive Guide for Practical Application in Early Intervention/Early Childhood Special Education.* Missoula, MT: Division for Early Childhood.

Sandall, S.R., I.S. Schwartz, G.E. Joseph, H.Y. Chou, E.M. Horn, J. Lieber, . . . R. Wolery. 2002. *Building Blocks for Teaching Preschoolers with Special Needs.* Baltimore: Brookes.

Sandall, S.R. & I.S. Schwartz. 2008. *Building Blocks for Teaching Preschoolers with Special Needs.* 2nd ed. Baltimore: Brookes.

Shapiro, E.S., N. Zigmond, T. Wallace, & D. Marston. 2011. *Models for Implementing Response to Intervention: Tools, Outcomes, and Implications.* New York: Guilford.

Sheridan, S.M., C.P. Edwards, C.A. Marvin, & L.L. Knoche. 2009. "Professional Development in Early Childhood Programs: Process Issues and Research Needs." *Early Education and Development* 20: 377–401.

Sheridan, S.M., C. Marvin, L. Knoche, & C.P. Edwards. 2008. "Getting Ready: Promoting School Readiness through a Relationship-Based Partnership Model." *Early Childhood Services, Special Issue on Young Children's Relationships* 2 (3): 149–72.

Slentz, K.L. & K.J. Hyatt. 2008. "Best Practices in Applying Curriculum-Based Assessment in Early Childhood." In volume 2 of *Best Practices in School Psychology V,* eds. A. Thomas & J. Grimes, 519–34. Bethesda, MD: National Association of School Psychologists.

Snyder, P., M.L. Hemmeter, & T. McLaughlin. 2011. "Professional Development in Early Childhood Intervention: Where We Stand on the Silver Anniversary of PL 99-457." *Journal of Early Intervention* 33 (4): 357–70.

Spencer, E., H. Goldstein, A. Sherman, S. Noe, R. Tabbah, R. Ziolkowski, & N. Schneider. In press. "Effects of an Automated Vocabulary and Comprehension Intervention: An Early Efficacy Study." *Journal of Learning Disabilities.*

Sugai, G. & R.H. Horner. 2009. "Responsiveness-to-Intervention and School-Wide Positive Behavior Supports: Integration of Multi-Tiered System Approaches." *Exceptionality: A Special Education Journal* 17 (4): 223–37. doi: 10.1080/09362830903235375.

Taba, H. 1962. *Curriculum Development Theory and Practice.* New York: Harcourt Brace & World.

Torgesen, J.K. 2009. "The Response to Intervention Instructional Model: Some Outcomes from a Large-Scale Implementation in Reading First Schools." *Child Development Perspectives* 3 (1): 38–40. doi:10.1111/j.1750-8606.2009.00073.x

US Department of Health and Human Services, Administration for Children and Families, Office of Head Start (HHS-ACF-OHS). 2011. *The Head Start Child Development and Early Learning Framework: Promoting Positive Outcomes in Early Childhood Programs Serving Children 3–5 Years Old.* Arlington, VA: Head Start Resource Center.

VanDerHeyden, A.M. & P. Snyder. 2006. "Integrating Frameworks from Early Childhood Intervention and School Psychology to Accelerate Growth for All Young Children." *School Psychology Review* 35 (4): 519–34.

VanDerHeyden, A.M., P. Snyder, C. Broussard, & K. Ramsdell. 2008. "Measuring Response to Early Literacy Intervention with Preschoolers At Risk." *Topics in Early Childhood Special Education* 27: 232–49.

Walker, H.M. & M.R. Shinn. 2010. "Systematic, Evidence-Based Approaches for Promoting Positive Student Outcomes within a Multi-Tier Framework: Moving from Efficacy to Effectiveness." In *Interventions for Achievement and Behavior Problems in a Three-Tier Model Including RTI,* eds. M.R. Shinn & H.M. Walker, 1–26. Washington, DC: National Association of School Psychologists.

Wolery, M. 2004. "Monitoring Child Progress." In *Assessing Infants and Preschoolers with Special Needs,* 3rd ed., eds. M. McLean, M. Wolery, & D.B. Bailey Jr., 545–84. Upper Saddle River, NJ: Prentice Hall.

Ysseldyke, J.E., M.L. Thurlow, & S.L. Christenson. 1987. *Teacher Effectiveness and Teacher Decision-Making: Implications for Effective Instruction of Handicapped Students.* Monograph no. 5, Instructional Alternatives Project. Minneapolis, MN: University of Minnesota.

Zaslow, M.J. 2009. "Strengthening the Conceptualization of Early Childhood Professional Development Initiatives and Evaluations." Report prepared for the US Department of Education. *Early Education and Development* 20 (3): 527–36.

Zaslow, M.J., K. Tout, T. Halle, J.V. Whittaker, & B. Lavelle. 2010. *Toward the Identification of Features of Effective Professional Development for Early Childhood Educators.* Washington, DC: Child Trends.

Suggested citation:

Division for Early Childhood, National Association for the Education of Young Children, & National Head Start Association, [DEC/NAEYC/NHSA]. (2013). *Frameworks for Response to Intervention in early childhood: Description and implications.* Missoula, MT: Author.

Writing Team

The following individuals served on the writing team for this paper. We thank them for their valuable contributions.

Kristie Pretti-Frontczak,
Chair Professor, Early Childhood Intervention College of Education, Health, and Human Services Kent State University

Judith J. Carta, PhD
Senior Scientist/Professor Juniper Gardens Children's Project/University of Kansas

Emmalie Dropkin, MA
Senior Specialist for Research and Policy National Head Start Association

Lise Fox, PhD
Professor and Director Florida Center for Inclusive Communities University of South Florida

Jennifer Grisham-Brown, EdD
Professor, Interdisciplinary Early Childhood Education Program Faculty Director, Early Childhood Laboratory University of Kentucky

Carolyn Pope Edwards, EdD
Willa Cather Professor
Departments of Psychology and
Child, Youth, and Family Studies
University of Nebraska–Lincoln

Susan Sandall, PhD
Professor, College of Education
Director, National Center on
Quality Teaching & Learning
University of Washington

Ashley N. Lyons, MEd
The Division for Early Childhood
Children's Action Network
Coordinator
Doctoral Student, Kent State
University

Patricia Snyder, PhD
Professor and David Lawrence
Jr. Endowed Chair in Early
Childhood Studies
University of Florida

Editors

Gera Jacobs, EdD
President, NAEYC Governing
Board Professor, Early Childhood
and Elementary Education
University of South Dakota

Together is Better: Environmental Teaching Practices to Support All Children's Learning

Philippa H. Campbell, Ph.D., OTR/L, FAOTA,
Thomas Jefferson University

Suzanne A. Milbourne, Ph.D., OTR/L,
University of Delaware

Recommended practice suggests three outcomes that are important for all young children's learning: (1) opportunities for children to learn and practice functional and developmental skills (Gestwicki, 1999; Wolery, 2005); (2) program structures that offer learning activities and routines that work well (Sandall & Schwartz, 2008); and (3) maximal participation in classroom activities and routines (National Association for the Education of Young Children [NAEYC] & Division for Early Childhood [DEC], 2009). Together these outcomes prepare all young children for future learning.

Teaching practices is the umbrella term used to describe what professionals do to help children participate in activities and routines and learn to use new skills. There are two general categories of teaching practices: instructional and environmental. Instructional practices include deciding what, when, and how to evaluate the effects of direct instruction, and how to promote and evaluate the quality of instruction provided by others (e.g., DEC, 2014; Epstein, 2014). Environmental practices refer to aspects of the space, materials (e.g., toys and books), equipment, routines, and activities that may intentionally be altered to support young children's learning (Copple, Bredekamp, Koralek, & Charner, 2013; DEC, 2014). Environmental practices encompass both the structural (space, equipment, and materials) and social (interactions with peers, siblings, family members) environments, whereas instructional practices create learning opportunities without reference to the specific learning context. For example, an adult may use physical guidance to help a child hold a spoon during lunch, a marker during art, or instruments during music.

Let's take a closer look at these two sets of complimentary teaching practices. As illustrated in Figure 1, the darker circles outline a process for making decisions about instructional practices. As a general rule, particularly in early childhood special education (ECSE) settings, children's skills are assessed, goals are established for new skill learning, instructional strategies are identified, and progress in skill learning is tracked. For children with disabilities, established goals may be listed on the infant's or toddler's Individual Family Service Plan (IFSP) or, for older children, on the Individualized Education Program (IEP). In most early childhood settings, instruction is used to provide opportunities for children to learn skills outlined in early learning standards or curricula. When adults instruct young children, they use strategies such as assistance, cueing, verbal direction, reflection, or other techniques generally provided by another person such as a teacher, parent, other adult, or peer.

Environmental practices include structural supports that help all children participate successfully in a classroom and include a variety of evidence-based strategies that support children's performance by impact-

Figure 1
Process for Making Decisions about Practices

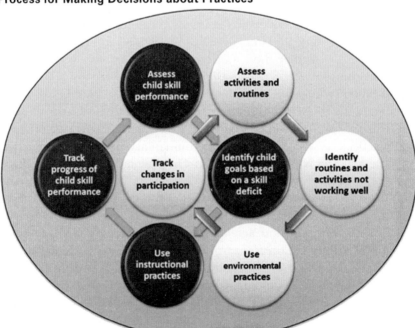

ing directly on the environment (Trivette, Dunst, Hamby, & O'Herin, 2010). Parents, teachers, and other professionals decide which types of environmental practices to try by using the process outlined on the white circles of Figure 1. This decision-making process begins by assessing the activities and routines occurring in the environment and identifying those that are not working as well as desired (e.g., Milbourne & Campbell, 2007). An activity or routine is not going well when an adult(s) is not satisfied with the activity or routine or a child is not participating as expected. Environmental practices are then implemented and changes in children's participation are tracked. When adults design and use environmental practices, they may use classroom-wide supports that work for all children, like a picture schedule and choice board, or child-specific supports, such as special chairs and switch-operated toys. Instructional and environmental practices, when blended together, result in an intentional and high-quality approach that is responsive to the needs of all children as well as differentiated for individual children's learning styles and abilities.

There are two general categories of teaching practices: instructional and environmental.

Ms. Regina commented: "We recently decided that I should step back a bit and let Katrina have time for self-play and time to interact with her classroom friends without my assistance." Katrina has significant physical disabilities and Ms. Regina spends time in the classroom providing one-on-one adult instruction and support. Ms. Regina used two types of environmental practices—(1) a recordable voice-output switch for communication, and (2) toys that Katrina

could manipulate—and provided adult support so that Katrina could sit and play. What she later realized was that she had inadvertently set up a situation where Katrina was not easily able to play and interact with anyone but Ms. Regina. By blending instructional and environmental practices, another child and Katrina were able to read a book together.

Instructional practices are widely used and common early childhood techniques have a direct impact on a child's performance. Adults show and tell how to do things so that children know what is expected. Practices used to provide instruction may be more commonly known than environmental practices. The purpose of this article is to provide information about environmental practices used as classroom-wide applications to support all children or as individually tailored supports to address the needs of a specific child. Environmental practices may be used alone or blended with instructional practices. A natural tendency for many adults is to help children by providing instruction through physical assistance, cueing, prompting, or even verbal direction—all of which are strategies delivered to a group of children or an individual child by another person, generally an adult. When an adult is using instructional practices with a child with a disability, the adult may only assist that one child, sometimes actually isolating the child from interactions with other children. Well-designed environmental practices reduce (and sometimes eliminate) the

need for one-on-one instruction above and beyond the level of instruction that is provided to other children in a classroom.

Ms. Sandra tried to help Jason participate in making an art project. The activity was very challenging. He did not like the sticky paste on his fingers and was unable to hold a paint brush. He resisted Ms. Sandra's attempts to provide hand-over-hand help. Ms. Talia stopped by the classroom to deliver some paperwork and saw what a hard time Ms. Sandra was having. Ms. Talia suggested using an environmental practice approach to design a different type of art activity to encourage child participation and eliminate the need for hand-over-hand instruction. Rather than touching the sticky paste, she suggested that Ms. Sandra modify the activity materials. Each child was given a plastic freezer bag containing several colors of paint allowing them to mix colors and create a painting without getting their hands in anything sticky.

Many labels describe the wide array of environmental practices that may be used to support young children's participation and learning. Some terms are used by particular disciplines but may mean the same thing. For example, in ECSE, terms such as visual support or assistive technology (AT) are used. In typical early learning settings, strategies such as room arrangement are strongly emphasized as environmental-based ways of helping all children whereas in ECSE, environmental modification is often a term used to describe supports for a particular child. An early childhood teacher might consider room arrangement in terms of providing a safe and healthy learning environment. Special education professionals might focus more on arranging a classroom to address an individual child's needs, for example, keeping the room arrangement consistent so that a child with impaired vision is able to navigate safely and independently.

Participation occurs when a child successfully engages in an activity with only the amount of adult support as is needed by most children.

Table 1 summarizes information and provides resource suggestions for five primary terms used to describe environmental practices. These terms include: (1) adaptations; (2) assistive technology; (3) visual supports; (4) universal design; and (5) universal design for learning (Campbell, Milbourne, & Wilcox, 2008). The terms represent the perspectives of different professional disciplines. For example, an early childhood teacher might view a picture schedule board as something used in many early childhood classrooms for all children, whereas a special educator might

Table 1
Terminology and Resources Associated with Environmental Practices

Term	Examples	Further Reading/Resources
Adaptations: Something that is altered, modified, or redesigned to make it suitable for a new use or purpose.	A classroom is redesigned to include picture exchange communication cards in all learning stations; a spoon is modified by wrapping the handle to enlarge the grip area; a ride-on toy is altered with PVC and pool noodles.	• Milbourne and Campbell (2007) • Campbell, Milbourne, and Kennedy (2012) • Head Start (2003)
Assistive technology: When a technology device is used to do something by a child with special needs that could otherwise not be done, the technology device is labeled "assistive technology."	Most children communicate using words, gestures, and facial expressions but a child with a disability may only be able to communicate by pointing to a picture, using a voice output device, or touching a tablet with a communication app.	• Tots N Tech Newsletters, http://tnt.asu.edu • Winton, Buysse, Rous, Epstein, and Pierce (2011) • NCDPI (2012a)
Visual supports: These effective supports may assist children in their ability to maintain attention, understand spoken language, and sequence and organize their environment. Includes: concrete items, pictures, symbols, printed words, and/or a combination of these.	Visual schedules, choice boards, first-then boards, cue cards, activity sequences, scripted stories, a feeling wheel, and a feeling chart.	• Lentini, Vaughn, and Fox (2008) • Hodgdon (1995)
Universal design: Creating physical environments that can be usable by all children without the need for adaptation. It also means that the environments are free from both physical and social barriers.	An entry with ramp access and automatic door openers to provide easy access for individuals with wheelchairs and parents with strollers; Equipment (toilets, sinks, chairs, tables, etc.) are of varying heights to accommodate all children.	• Financial and Design Solutions for the Development of Inclusive Child Care Centers, http://www.easterseals.com • The Universal Design of Early Education: Moving forward for All Children, http://www.naeyc.org • NCDPI (2012b) • Center for Universal Design (1997)

Table 1 (continued)

Term	Examples	Further Reading/Resources
Universal design for learning: Designing early education learning opportunities so all children, as equal and valued members of the program, may access and engage in all learning opportunities, learn from a common curriculum according to their individual strengths and abilities, and demonstrate their learning in multiple ways.	Present content in multiple formats, including verbal, print, video, or concrete objects, repeating key words/phrases in children's home language and using simple sentences with gestures.	• Conn-Powers, Cross, Traub, and Hutter-Pishgahi (2006) • Building Inclusive Child Care (BICC) http://www.northampton.edu/early-childhood-education/partnerships/building-inclusive-child-care.htm • Center for Applied Special Technology (2013)

think about a picture schedule as specially designed visual support for a child with challenging behavior, intellectual disability, or autism.

Figure 2 illustrates how environmental practices build in complexity and specialization from a foundational to a top tier (e.g., Campbell, 2012). The Tier 1 foundation is based on universal design and universal design for learning perspectives and consists of environmental practices appropriate for any child, with or without a special need. In early childhood classrooms, these foundational practices are described as classroom-wide supports and might include using child-sized chairs so that all children may sit with their feet on the floor. In Tier 2, explicit adaptations to the environment, schedule, activity, or materials to enable children to participate successfully are represented. Adaptations are appropriate for all children but are especially helpful when addressing individual child learning needs. For example, some toddlers may be more successful when drinking from a sippy, rather than a regular, cup; others may do better with a cup with two handles rather than with no handles. Tier 3 consists of highly specialized and individualized devices used to address children's needs to perform functional skills, learn, and participate. For example, a child with significant motor disability may move around the environment in a highly specialized power chair tailored to that individual child's needs. Another young child with less severe mobility restrictions may use a Tier 2 adaptation of a modified commercially available toy jeep. Very few children require the highly individual-

Figure 2
Environmental Practices Decision Making for All Children across Settings

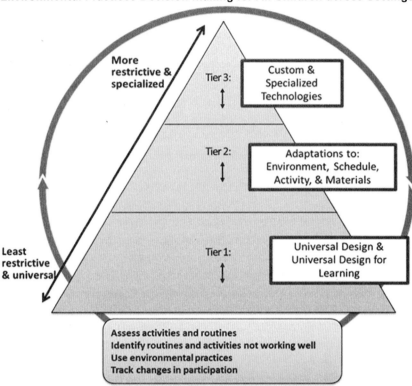

ized and specialized devices at the Tier 3 environmental practice level but many children's participation and performance are increased with use of Tier 1 or Tier 2 environmental practices.

The tiered perspective outlined in Figure 2 includes AT devices in Tiers 2 and 3. AT is a different but complimentary concept to universal design; however, in contrast to universal design, AT relates specifically to people with disabilities. Many people think of AT only as expensive, high technology devices like computerized communication aids even though an AT device is defined in IDEA as "any item, piece of equipment or product system, whether acquired commercially off the shelf, modified, or customized, that is used to increase, maintain, or improve the functional capabilities of children with disabilities" (Authority 20 U.S.C. 1401[1]). AT may be as simple as adapting a marker by wrapping it in duct tape so that it is easier to hold or as specialized as a custom designed power wheelchair that is operated by head movement. AT ranges on a continuum from very low technology devices such as the adapted marker to highly

Table 2
Companion Core Principles of RTI and Environment-Based Instruction

Among the core principles of RTI that align with recommended practice in early childhood are the following:	Among the core principles of environmental practices that align with RIT core principles are the following:
• Specification of a multitiered system of supports	• Specification of a hierarchy of decision making
• Early provision of support or intentional teaching/caregiving with sufficient intensity to promote positive outcomes and prevent later problems	• Intentional use of levels of a hierarchy to assure the use of least restrictive levels first to promote positive outcomes and enable participation
• Use of child data to inform teaching and responsive caregiving practices	• Use of adult perceptions and perspective to inform the enhancement of activities and routines

specialized, individualized, and custom devices that generally are both high technology and expensive.

In early childhood education programs, shifts are occurring from a skill-learning emphasis to a broader focus on children's participation in classroom activities and routines. A solid evidence-based foundation supports the idea that a focus on participation is equally as important as a focus on skill development (Rosenberg, Bart, Ratzon & Jarus, 2013; Maxwell, 2007; Evans, 2006; Legendre, 2003). Participation occurs when a child successfully engages in an activity with only the amount of adult support as is needed by most children. Some children may participate successfully with just universal or classroom-wide supports (Tier 1) while others may need individualized supports (Tiers 2 and 3) to fully participate in classroom activities and routines. Participation is the act of taking part or sharing in something. Participation occurs throughout the day, for example, when children choose songs during morning meeting, pour milk during lunch, wait in line to go down the sliding board, or help friends fasten their coats. Participation describes the child's action (i.e., what the child does such as request a song), not how the action is accomplished. In other words, a child who chooses a song (i.e., the action or what the child does) during morning meeting with a communication device, by signing, or pointing to a choice board (i.e., how the action is accomplished) is participating in selecting songs just as is a child who is able to verbally request the song. When early childhood educators intentionally plan, environmental practices may be used as classroom-wide applications to support all children or as individually tailored supports to address the needs of a specific child (Campbell, Milbourne, & Kennedy, 2012; Milbourne & Campbell, 2007).

Using Classroom-Wide Environmental Practices

Settings such as children's homes, schools, or child-care facilities are characterized by routines and activities, all of which offer opportunities for participation. For example, bath time is less likely to occur in a child's school than in the home. But other routines, such as mealtime or toileting will occur in many different settings. Most early learning settings are organized with classroom routines such as coming to or leaving school, transition, or mealtimes such as snack, breakfast, or lunch. These routines occur every day in most early childhood programs. These types of programs also offer activities in which opportunities for children's participation and learning are embedded. Activities may vary by the age of the children, their interests, the length of time they are likely to be engaged, the curriculum or learning standards underlying the activities, or other similar factors. Activities such as morning meeting/circle, learning centers, art, music, or storybook reading are included in most early learning programs.

Environmental practices impact child performance indirectly by modifying or adapting the structural environment rather than by directly targeting a child as does an instructional practice such as hand-over-hand spoon feeding.

The structural environment of early childhood settings is shaped by the adults who design them. Educators arrange furniture and equipment, create daily schedules, choose and create activities, display and offer a variety of materials, and provide adult assistance. They plan adult-directed activities and provide time for unplanned (i.e., incidental) learning opportunities. When using environmental practices, adults consider how the environment supports or interferes with children's opportunities for learning and participation. Environmental practices are used to address outcomes for child learning, including establishing program structures where learning activities work well, providing opportunities for children to learn, and maximizing participation in classroom activities and routines. A primary outcome of the use of environmental practices is to increase children's participation. Environmental practices impact child performance indirectly by modifying or adapting the structural environment rather than by directly targeting a child as does an instructional practice such as hand-over-hand spoon-feeding.

Ms. Ruby was concerned about children's transitions and wanted her classroom structure to support children's successful participation in transition. She was also worried about one student whose fine motor skills were not as good as expected for his age. Picking up or manipulating small objects was hard for Noah. He had so much difficulty with manipulation that he frequently removed himself from activities involving small objects. Ms. Ruby used a classroom picture schedule, a classroom-wide environmental practice, to help all of the children in her room know about classroom activities and routines. She increased learning opportunities for Noah to practice manipulation by asking him to display the current activity in the classroom. She pasted Velcro squares on the picture schedule and gave Noah a small foam ball that he placed next to the correct activity each time the activity changed. All children's transitions were better because they saw what was going to happen next.

Classroom-wide environmental practices include actions such as conscious arrangement of the classroom so that children know expectations such as to be quiet in the reading nook and use of adaptations such as picture schedules, choice boards, or other ways of providing children nonverbal information about expectations. Ms. Ruby got interested in using classroom-wide supports after she tried a picture schedule (e.g., visual support) and it worked. She reported that she no longer felt as if she were having to "repeat and repeat and repeat." She and the children made a chart for their classroom rules and another for choices about learning

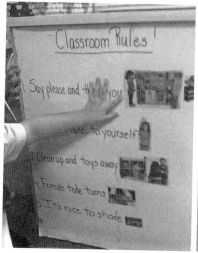
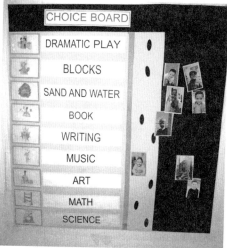

center activities. . The picture charts helped all of the children understand classroom expectations.

"Blocks always seem like they should be a good activity for children," Ms. Tanisha commented to a parent who visited her classroom, *"but here's the situation—the children use them to hit each other or throw them like missiles. I know I am supposed to have a block corner but I want to take these away."* The parent observed the children playing and then she suggested things to manage the situation that she had seen in her child's previously attended preschool. The final solution involved a visual support in the block center to remind the children about objects they could build and how many children could be present.

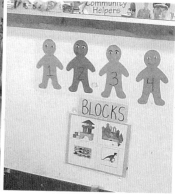

Using Environmental Practices with Individual Children

Individual children may benefit from the specially designed environmental practices (Campbell & Wilcox, 2012). A first step is to determine the status of activities and routines (see Campbell, 2011; Milbourne & Campbell, 2007 for suggested checklists). An activity or routine is not going well when an adult(s) is not satisfied with a particular activity or routine or a child is not participating as expected. When an activity or routine is not going well, the model of tiered environmental practices (i.e., Figure 2) guides the design of the number and types of practices that may be tried.

Classroom observation showed that Ms. Regina, the paraprofessional assigned to Katrina, provided a high level of adult assistance. Ms. Regina worried that if she "stepped back," Katrina would not be able to participate because she needed almost 100% adult assistance. Using the environmental tiered model, Tier 1 foundation practices were identified to set up the environment around Katrina to promote participation. All children's chairs were placed in a large space around a large table. Ms. Regina was positioned off to the side away from Katrina and the other children but available to facilitate social interaction or help, as necessary. These Tier 1 practices were expanded by adding Tier 2 and 3 practices. Katrina used an adapted cup (Tier 2). Highly specialized adaptive seating (Tier 3) was designed to maintain her at the same table height as her classmates but also provide supports so that she would have maximal use of her arms. Katrina was able to interact with the other children while eating and drinking with

minimal use of adult-facilitation and maximal use of environment-based practices.

This scenario illustrates the differences between instructional and environmental practices. Without an adapted chair, an adult would have to hold Katrina. Without adapted utensils and a cup, an adult would have to feed her. Just these two situations would be likely to inadvertently isolate her from other children. She would require 100% adult assistance and have virtually no opportunities to participate independently in eating or socializing. In all likelihood, Katrina will require adult-provided instructional practices to help her improve motor patterns for eating and drinking, but these may be blended with environmental practices by providing the instructional practices on top of the environmental practices that are already in place, thereby reducing the amount of adult instruction necessary. One additional situation further illustrates the differences between instructional and environmental practices.

Ms. Regina wondered about helping Katrina to participate without always needing adult assistance. After all, Ms. Regina provided one-on-one assistance because Katrina was unable to do things on her own. Even though she knew about room arrangement, Ms. Regina did not think these ideas applied to Katrina. When the occupational therapist (OT) visited the classroom, Ms. Regina asked her about Katrina's need for adult assistance. The OT and Ms. Regina shared their perspectives and worked out a way to use a large pillow to support Katrina so that she would be able to practice sitting independently during story time. They also worked together to rearrange the room to provide enough open space so that Katrina could practice walking by navigating her gait trainer in the classroom.

Summary

Environmental practices may be provided as classroom-wide applications to support all children or be individually tailored to address the needs of a specific child; they may be used alone or blended with instructional practices provided to groups or individual children by another person. Uses of environmental practices were described in this article with examples of their use with groups or individual children. This type of instruction seems like noninstruction, but systematic reviews about the use of adaptations (Tier 2) and AT (Tier 3) demonstrate a strong evidence-base supporting use of environmental practices to promote participation and learning. Because environmental practices do not require an adult to use strategies such as physical assistance, cueing, or verbal direction, teachers and other professionals often have questions about the validity of these practices.

Environmental practices may be provided as classroom-wide applications to support all children or be individually tailored to address the needs of a specific child.

Frequently Asked Questions

- *May practices associated with each of the tiers in Figure 2 be combined?*

Absolutely! The tiers of the triangle were created to assist with planning and ensure that a variety of environmental practices are considered. For example, Katrina uses a specialized chair (Tier 3) a sippy cup (Tier 2), and environmental arrangement (Tier 1). Recall that the environmental practice tiers are useful for children with and without disabilities across early childhood settings.

- *How long should something be tried?*

Another way to ask this question is—how will I know when the environmental practice is working? When on-going assessments of participation are conducted—for example, Ms. Regina wrote down the amount of liquid that Katrina drank by herself from the cup each day—the change in participation will govern whether and when new practices are needed.

- *What happens when something that was successful is no longer working?*

When an environmental practice is no longer needed, this may mean that enough opportunity for participation was provided and that the child (or children) has met participation expectations for that activity or routine without need of ongoing support. It may also mean that the introduction of new or different type of environmental practice may be necessary to continue to support the child's new learning.

- *Who is responsible for making no- and low-tech adaptations/AT (Tier 1 and 2)?*

Anyone who sees an opportunity to introduce environmental practices can find or make the needed adaptations or materials. A liability of low-tech adaptations/AT is that someone has to actually make them. This person may be classroom personnel, therapy staff, or volunteers.

- *Do I have to be a speech and language pathologist to make a picture choice board (Tier 1)?*

No! Simple picture choice boards are easy to make using photos of children or pictures cut from magazines or catalogs. Two important aspects to remember are to consider how many choices are provided at one time and how you want to organize the picture choice board for the most flexibility.

- *What do I do with an item once a child no longer needs it?*

The more complex an item may be, the more likely that another child may be able to use it. There may be a local lending library or AT exchange or recycle program that will take the item, you might store it for another child, or take a photo of the item and post it in local publications for sale.

- *If we make/buy an item for a child's classroom can the child use it at home?*

Most certainly! Consider a simple choice board for mealtime—it can be used in the classroom, at home, and in a restaurant. If it is a no- or low-tech item, perhaps making more than one will be helpful.

- *When a child has an IFSP or an IEP are there special considerations to using an environmental practices?*

A child's IFSP/IEP team should consult local guidelines regarding the purchase, sharing, and storing of any items being used, particularly when the items are expensive. Many school districts or EI agencies have developed policies, particularly as related to AT. Teams should intentionally link practices used to teach IFSP outcomes with those used to teach IEP goals and make specific plans for the use of items such as adaptations/AT across all settings.

- *Is it appropriate to ask a child's family to contribute ideas for classroom adaptations?*

Families may be using adaptations, devices, or strategies at home that may be helpful in the classroom (or visa-versa). Families are an important part of any team that is planning to promote a child's participation in everyday activities and routines. Families often teach other families about using adaptations—so why not ask them to teach you! Although what is used with their children may not be labeled as an adaptation, support, or AT, families make attempts to promote a child's participation in family events, celebrations, activities, and gatherings and are often naturally using an approach of environment-based instruction.

Note

For more information, please contact Philippa H. Campbell at pipcamp@aol.com

References

Building Inclusive Child Care (BICC) Retrieved June 26, 2014, from http://www.northampton.edu/early-childhood-education/partnerships/building-inclusive-child-care.htm

Campbell, P. H. (2011). Using the assessment of family activities and routines to develop embedded programming. *Young Exceptional Children* (Monograph Series No. 13: Gathering Information to Make Informed Decisions, pp. 64-78). Missoula, MT: Division for Early Childhood of the Council of Exceptional Children.

Campbell, P. H. (2012). Occupational and physical therapy. In M. Batshaw, N. J. Roizen, & G. R. Lotrecchiano, (Eds.), *Children with disabilities* (7th ed., pp. 599-612). Baltimore: Paul H. Brookes.

Campbell, P. H., Milbourne, S. A., & Kennedy, A. A. (2012). *CARA's kit for toddlers.* Baltimore: Paul H. Brookes.

Campbell, P. H., Milbourne, S. A., & Wilcox, M. J. (2008). Adaptation interventions to promote participation in natural settings. *Infants and Young Children, 21*(2), 94–106.

Campbell, P. H. & Wilcox, M. J. (2012). Using assistive technology to promote inclusion in early childhood settings. In L. Mucio (Ed.), *Spotlight on technology.* Washington, DC: NAEYC.

Center for Applied Special Technology. (2013). *About universal design for learning.* Retrieved June 26, 2014, from http://www.cast.org/udl/index.html

Center for Universal Design. (1997). *About UD: Universal design principles.* Raleigh, NC: North Carolina State University. Retrieved June 26, 2014, from http://www.ncsu.edu/ncsu/design/cud/about_ud/udprinciples.htm

Conn-Powers, M., Cross, A. F., Traub, E. K., & Hutter-Pishgahi, L. (2006, September). The universal design of early education: Moving forward for all children. *Beyond the Journal: Young Children on the Web.* Retrieved from June 26, 2014, http://www.naeyc.org/files/yc/file/200609/ConnPowersBTJ.pdf

Copple, C., Bredekamp, S., Koralek, D., & Charmer, K. (2013). *Developmentally appropriate practice: Focus on preschoolers.* Washington, DC: NAEYC.

Division for Early Childhood. (2014). DEC recommended practices in early intervention/early childhood special education. Retrieved from http://www.dec-sped.org/recommendedpractices

Epstein, A. S. (2014). *The intentional teacher: Choosing the best strategies for young children's learning* (Rev ed.). Washington, DC: NAEYC.

Evans, G. W. (2006). Child development and the physical environment. *Annual Review of Psychology, 57*: 423–452.

Financial and Design Solutions for the Development of Inclusive Child Care Centers. Retrieved June 26, 2014, from http://www.easterseals.com/explore-resources/making-life-accessible/financial-and-design.html

Gestwicki, C. (1999). *Developmentally appropriate practice: Curriculum and development in early education*. Albany, NY: Delmar.

Head Start. (2003). Adaptations for individual children: Adaptations for children with disabilities. *The Head Start leaders guide to positive child outcomes*. HHS/ACF/ACYF/HSB. Retrieved from http://eclkc.ohs.acf.hhs.gov/

Hodgdon, L. (1995). *Visual strategies for improving communication practical supports for school and home*. Troy: Quirk Roberts.

Individuals with Disabilities Education Improvement Act of 2004, Authority 20 USC 1401(1).

Legendre, A. (2003). Environmental features influencing toddlers' bioemotional reactions in day care centers. *Environment & Behavior, 35*(4), 523–549.

Lentini, R., Vaughn, B. J., & Fox, L. (2008). *Creating teaching tools for young children with challenging behavior. Folder 5—Visual Strategies*. Retrieved June 26, 2014, from http://challengingbehavior.fmhi.usf.edu/do/resources/teaching_tools/ttyc_toc.htm.

Maxwell, L. E. (2007). Competency in child care settings: The role of the physical environment. *Environment & Behavior, 39* (2), 229–245.

Milbourne, S. A. & Campbell, P. H. (2007). *CARA's kit for preschoolers (Teacher and consultant guides)*. Philadelphia: Thomas Jefferson University.

National Association for the Education of Young Children & Division for Early Childhood. (2009). *Early childhood inclusion: A joint position statement of the Division for Early Childhood and the National Association for the Education of Young Children*. Chapel Hill: University of North Carolina, FPG Child Development Institute. Retrieved June 26, 2014, from http://www.naeyc.org/files/naeyc/file/positions/DEC_NAEYC_EC_updatedKS.pdf

National Professional Development Center on Inclusion. (2012a). *Quality inclusive practices: Resources and learning pads. Assistive technology*. Retrieved June 26, 2014, from http://npdci.fpg.unc.edu/assistive-technology

National Professional Development Center on Inclusion. (2012b). *Quality inclusive practices: Resources and learning pads. Universal design*. Retrieved June 26, 2014, from http://npdci.fpg.unc.edu/universal-design-ud-universal-design-learning-udl

Northampton Community College. (2007). *Building inclusive child care: Universal design for learning* (video). Retrieved June 26, 2014, from http://www.northampton.edu/early-childhood-education/partnerships/building-inclusive-child-care.htm

Rosenberg, L., Bart, O., Ratzon, N. Z., & Jarus, T. (2013). Personal and environmental factors predict participation of children with and without mild developmental disabilities. *Journal of Child & Family Studies, 22*(5), 658–671.

Sandall, S. R. & Schwartz, I. S. (2008). *Building blocks for teaching children with special needs*. Baltimore: Paul H. Brookes.

Trivette, C. M, Dunst, C J., Hamby, D. W., & O'Herin, C. E. (2010). Effects of different types of adaptations on the behavior of young children with disabilities. *Research Brief, 4*(1), 1–26. Retrieved June 26, 2014, from http://tnt.asu.edu/files/Adaptaqtions_Brief_final.pdf

Winton, P., Buysse, V., Rous, B., Epstein, D., & Pierce, P. (2011). CONNECT Module 5: Assistive Technology Interventions [Web-based professional development curriculum]. Chapel Hill: University of North Carolina, FPG Child Development Institute. Retrieved June 26, 2014, from http://community.fpg.unc.edu/connect-modules/learners/module-5

Wolery, M. (2005) DEC recommended practices: Child-focused practices. In S. Sandall, M. L. Hemmeter, B. S. Smith, & M. B. McLean (Eds), *DEC recommended practices: A comprehensive guide for practical application in early intervention/early childhood special education* (pp. 71–106). Longmont, CO: Sopris West.

Adapting Lesson Plans for Preschoolers

Addressing State Early Learning Standards

Emily Dorsey, M.Ed.,

Natalie Danner, M.A., M.S.E.,

Bernadette Laumann, Ph.D.
University of Illinois at Urbana-Champaign

Ms. Jones is a licensed early childhood teacher working in a state-funded preschool classroom for students who have diverse learning needs. Her state recently adopted a revised set of early learning and development standards that align with the state common core standards (K–12). Ms. Jones, along with her teaching assistant, Ms. Hernandez, is responsible for addressing these standards. She is concerned about how to meet the needs of all children in her classroom while blending developmentally appropriate best practices for all children with specialized instruction for children with disabilities or special learning needs.

Ms. Jones's classroom serves fifteen 3- to 5-year-olds with diverse backgrounds and learning needs. Most of them are typically developing with age-appropriate skills and behaviors; however, two children, Joey and Hailey, have special needs requiring individual education programs (IEPs). Joey has a developmental delay and Down syndrome. He often needs more support with academic tasks and self-help skills. Hailey has cerebral palsy (CP) resulting in significant motor delays, especially on the left side of her body. She uses a wheelchair for mobility. Ms. Jones has also started to notice that Aiden, a child without an IEP or diagnosed disability, often exhibits challenging behavior during transition and wait times.

The children in Ms. Jones's classroom are about to begin working on a project about shoe stores. Project work is "a child-initiated, firsthand,

in-depth investigation on a topic of interest undertaken by a group of children" (Beneke & Ostrosky, 2013, p. 23). Ms. Jones has already begun incorporating elements of this project into her classroom environment and activities. For example, the dramatic play area is set up as a shoe store with a cash register, money, a bench, shoes, shoeboxes, and shopping bags. The book center now contains nonfiction books about shoes worn around the world. The art center has shoes nearby that children can use as models for still life paintings of shoes. The science center also contains shoes of varying sizes, with tools for measuring and weighing them.

Ms. Jones has taken the children on a field trip to a local shoe store and has invited a classroom parent who works as a salesperson at that same shoe store to come speak to the class.

Ms. Jones is excited to see children actively engaged in relevant learning activities within the context of the shoe store project, but she feels intimidated about incorporating meaningful lessons that address her state's early learning standards. She is also concerned about making lessons accessible to all children. She knows that she may need to make some adaptations but is not sure when or how to do that. Ms. Jones decides to invite a few other teachers and teaching assistants to her classroom for a brainstorming session one day after school, hoping to come up with a planning process that will benefit everyone.

Learning to adapt lesson plans to meet individual children's needs is an important skill for classroom teachers, teacher educators, and professional development providers to have in their toolbox (Sandall & Schwartz, 2008). The goal of this article is to provide early childhood professionals working in inclusive early childhood environments with a process for adapting lesson plans to meet the individual needs and goals of children (with and without disabilities) while addressing state early learning standards. In this article, we first present relevant background information about inclusive early childhood environments, early learning standards, and strategies to serve diverse learners. Following this review of the literature, we continue the storyline introduced in the opening vignette to illustrate the process one teacher used to develop individualized, developmentally appropriate lesson plans that align with her state's early learning standards. Throughout the article, tools are provided to help teachers develop and adapt their lesson plans to support learning opportunities that address children's individual goals.

Ms. Jones is excited to see children actively engaged in relevant learning activities within the context of the shoe store project, but she feels intimidated about incorporating meaningful lessons that address her state's early learning standards.

Inclusive Early Childhood Environments

Professionals in early care and education recognize the importance of providing inclusive preschool placements for young children (Division for Early Childhood [DEC]/National Association for the Education of Young Children [NAEYC], 2009). Most preschoolers with disabilities are enrolled in inclusive programs such as public pre-K, Head Start, or child care (U.S. Department of Education, 2012). These programs use a variety of curriculum models and instructional strategies, including large- and small-group instruction and project work.

However, to create a truly inclusive environment, all children, including children with disabilities, must have meaningful access to learning activities. According to Beneke and Ostrosky (2013), "Early childhood educators understand the importance of building a classroom community of diverse learners and their families, and they know it is important to find approaches that provide access to learning experiences in which all children can fully participate while receiving individualized support" (p. 23). LaRoque and Darling (2008) also emphasize the importance of general education teachers being able to individualize and adapt lessons to meet the needs of all learners.

Early Learning Standards

To promote high-quality early childhood programs, many states have created early learning standards. According to the National Center on Child Care Quality Improvement (2013), "All 50 states and six territories have developed ELGs [early learning guidelines] for children birth to five years, and virtually all have ELGs for infants and toddlers" (p. 1). Teachers in inclusive settings are faced with multiple challenges: providing a high-quality early childhood environment, aligning curriculum to address state early learning standards, and meeting the needs of diverse learners. Fortunately, several states are providing guidance about how to use standards with children who have disabilities (Scott-Little, Lesko, Martella, & Milburn, 2007). For a comprehensive list of states and territories that have adopted early learning guidelines, visit the following Web site by the National Center on Child Care Quality Improvement: https://childcareta. acf.hhs.gov/sites/default/files/075_1301_state_elgs_web_0.pdf.

Early learning standards can be a valuable part of a comprehensive, high-quality system of services for young children. These standards can define the desired outcomes and content of young children's education (NAEYC, 2009). One state has argued that the purpose (of standards) is to assist the early childhood community in providing high-quality programs and services for children age 3 years to kindergarten enrollment (Illinois State Board of Education, 2013).

Standards are often organized under broad subject domains such as language arts, math, science, and social studies. In Illinois, an example of a language arts standard is "use language to convey information and ideas." An example of a math standard is "demonstrate beginning understanding of numbers, number names, and numerals." Standards may be further broken down into individual benchmarks (Illinois State Board of Education, 2013). Standards contain important information for teachers, and it is essential that standards be incorporated into the classroom in meaningful ways. Rather than blindly putting together activities to meet the state early learning standards, it is critical for early childhood teachers to plan for and intentionally provide young children with essential experiences (Katz, 2014).

When considering what state early learning standards are, it is equally as important to address what they are not. Some misconceptions exist about how standards should be used. To be clear, early learning standards are not (1) an assessment, (2) a curriculum, or (3) a skill checklist (Gebhard, 2010). They are to be used as an important part of a "comprehensive, high quality system of services for young children" (NAEYC & National Association of Early Childhood Specialists in State Departments of Education, 2009).

Early learning standards should apply to all young children, regardless of ability level. However, adaptations may be necessary for some children to access and participate in the typical classroom activities that align with state standards. One state highlights why it is important to use early learning standards in inclusive classrooms and with children with disabilities.

Some children may have an identified developmental delay or disability that may require teachers to adapt the expectations set out in the standards and to make accommodations in experiences. Goals set for children who have an IEP reflect these adaptations and accommodations so that individual children can be supported as they work toward particular preschool benchmarks (Illinois State Board of Education, 2013, p. 16).

> *Early learning standards should apply to all young children, regardless of ability level. However, adaptations may be necessary for some children to access and participate in the typical classroom activities that align with state standards.*

Strategies to Serve Diverse Learners

The Individuals With Disabilities Education Act (IDEA) of 2004 is federal legislation mandating that schools provide services for young children with disabilities in the least restrictive environment. This means that children with disabilities should be educated to the maximum extent appropriate alongside peers without disabilities (Yell, 2006). For most young children, the least restrictive environment is an inclusive general education preschool classroom. An inclusive preschool setting should offer a high-quality program that includes typically developing children working alongside children with disabilities and meets the needs of children with disabilities through specialized support for active participation in activities and routines (Schwartz, Sandall, Odom, Horn, & Beckman, 2002).

Providing inclusive educational experiences for young children is a priority for the field of early care and education. Recognizing this priority, two national organizations, DEC and NAEYC, developed a joint position statement on early childhood inclusion in 2009. This joint position statement describes three defining features of inclusion: (1) children's *access* to a wide range of learning opportunities and environments, (2) children's *participation* in classroom routines and activities through scaffolded learning, and (3) the provision of system-level *supports* such as professional development, opportunities for collaboration, and sufficient funding. Thus, although the definition of early childhood inclusion has been evolving for several decades (Odom, Buysse, & Soukakou, 2011), DEC/NAEYC's joint position statement provides direction and guidance for the design of programs blending best practices in early childhood education for all children with best practices in specialized instruction for children with disabilities.

Developmentally appropriate practice (DAP) is a framework that has been developed by NAEYC. Principles of DAP can be applied in the development of high-quality, inclusive programs for young children, as described by DEC/NAEYC (2009). Within a DAP framework, teachers get to know children in a meaningful way, considering their age, developmental status, and cultural context. Teachers use that information, coupled with their knowledge of curriculum development and intentional teaching, to plan challenging yet achievable activities (NAEYC, 2009).

DEC believes in the rights of all children, regardless of their abilities, to participate meaningfully within their communities. Thus, high-quality, inclusive preschool programs must also consider specialized practices for children with disabilities or other diverse learning needs. These specialized, child-focused practices comprise three main components. First, adults design environments to promote children's safety, active engagement, learning, participation, and membership. Second, adults use ongoing data to individualize and adapt their practice to meet each child's changing needs. Third, adults use systematic procedures within and across environments, activities, and routines to promote children's learning and participation (DEC, 2014).

Combining the core principles of DAP for all children with DEC's recommended practices for children with diverse learning needs may seem intimidating. However, teachers can often make simple adaptations to the classroom environment, materials, lessons, and activities and embed individualized learning goals to support all children as meaningful participants in the learning community. It is important that teachers not feel isolated in their endeavor to create inclusive classrooms. Winton, McCollum, and Catlett (2008) describe several ways in which teachers can collaborate with one another, including coaching, consultation, reflective supervision, teaming, and communities of practice. Some teachers may choose to collaborate informally by calling a meeting of other staff members for a brainstorming session or by joining an online discussion group

Table 1
Questions to Consider in Creating an Inclusive Early Childhood Classroom

First steps: Foundations for a high-quality inclusive classroom	Next steps: Foundations of adapted lesson planning
Are you familiar with your state's early learning standards?[a]	Are you tying your lesson plan to your state's early learning standards?
Does your classroom or program welcome children who vary in culture, language, socioeconomic background, and ability?	Will the lesson you are planning be available to all children in the classroom?
Are you implementing high-quality, developmentally appropriate practices in your classroom?	Does your lesson describe a learning activity that is meaningful, relevant, and engaging to young children?
Does your preschool program/classroom environment reflect the three core components of DEC/NAEYC's (2009) joint position statement on inclusion?	Are you adapting your lesson plans to meet the needs of individual children?
Do all children have access to a wide range of learning opportunities and environments?	Is the lesson you are planning accessible to all children in the classroom or small group?
Do all children participate in classroom routines and activities through scaffolded learning?	Have you made adaptations or accommodations for individual children, allowing them to meaningfully participate in the lesson?
Do you have system-level supports for the inclusion of all children (e.g., professional development, opportunities for collaboration, sufficient funding)?	Have you embedded individual children's IEP goals into the lesson plan?
Do you collaborate formally and/or informally with other professionals and parents?	Have you developed or discussed your lesson plan with a trusted collaborator?

Note. See Scott-Little, Lesko, Martella, and Milburn (2007) for information about early learning guidelines. Refer to the following resources for information about inclusive preschool environments: Division for Early Childhood (DEC) and National Association for Young Children (NAEYC) (2009); National Association for the Education of Young Children (2009); Division for Early Childhood (2014). Refer to the following resources for information about lesson planning: Grisham-Brown, Hemmeter, and Pretti-Frontczak (2005); LaRoque and Darling (2008); Sandall and Schwartz (2008). See Winton, McCollum, and Catlett (2008) for information about collaboration. IEP = individualized education program.

on a topic of interest. Parents can be an excellent collaborative resource, able to offer suggestions of instructional strategies and adaptations that work best for their child (Grisham-Brown, Hemmeter, & Pretti-Frontczak, 2005). Teachers may not have access to every form of collaborative relationship described here but can work within their resources to form meaningful partnerships that support inclusion in their classroom.

As preschool teachers engage in the process of planning to meet the needs of diverse learners, it may be helpful to refer to a set of guiding questions to stimulate reflection about what it means to create a truly inclusive community of learners. The checklist *Questions to Consider in Creating an Inclusive Early Childhood Classroom* (see Table 1) may assist teachers with this process. This checklist addresses critical principles noted in this article (inclusive early childhood environments, early learning standards, strategies to serve diverse learners) and may help teachers reflect on the ways those principles can be applied in their own settings.

Teachers should first consider the items on the left side of the checklist. These items target the underlying foundations of an inclusive classroom. As teachers create individual lessons, the next part of the process described in the remainder of this article, they can consider questions on the right side of the checklist. Teachers will want to discuss this checklist with a trusted collaborator, who may help identify potential barriers to inclusion and think of creative solutions to overcome those barriers.

Adapting Lesson Plans

After brainstorming with the other preschool teachers and teaching assistants at her school, Ms. Jones feels ready to tackle her first adapted activity addressing a benchmark of her state's early learning standards. Knowing that the shoe store project is a relevant and meaningful context for instruction, Ms. Jones decides to plan a small-group lesson related to shoes. This lesson will occur at the art center and will target the following language arts benchmark: "Children will describe familiar places, things, and events and, with teacher assistance, provide additional detail."

The small-group lesson Ms. Jones plans involves children noticing and recalling information about their own shoes (e.g., color, shape, size, where they are located at home, who assists them with putting on or tying their shoes). Children will create paintings of their shoes on easels in the art center. As they are painting, Ms. Jones will elicit descriptions from the children by prompting them with questions and other conversation starters. She will use labels, dictations, and photo-

graphs to record information that children share about their paintings. (See Table 2 for a comprehensive description of Ms. Jones's lesson.)

Ms. Jones feels pleased with how her lesson will incorporate project work as well as align with the state's language arts benchmark, but she is still concerned about ensuring that all children will be able to meaningfully participate in the lesson. Ms. Jones sits down with her teaching assistant, Ms. Hernandez, to talk about each child who will

Table 2
Original Lesson Plan

Language Arts benchmark

Children will describe familiar places, things, and events and, with teacher assistance, provide additional detail.

Activity (10–12 minutes)

Teacher will facilitate discussion and artistic representation of shoes during a small group art activity. Conversation will focus on the children's shoes, on the location of shoes in their homes, and on how people help children put on and tie their shoes. Children will create paintings of their shoes as they talk.

Materials

• Child's own shoe

• Easel

• Paper

• Paint (variety of colors) in containers

• Paintbrushes (variety of sizes)

Procedure

1. To introduce the small-group art activity, Ms. Jones models the lesson during large-group time. She removes one shoe, holds it up for the class, and describes it, saying "Here is my black shoe. It has laces. I get my shoes from my bedroom closet each morning. I put them on and tie them all by myself."

(Before large-group time began, Ms. Jones placed an easel next to the large-group area, along with a few containers of paint and several paintbrushes.) She now models the painting activity, narrating her actions as she works. She says, "I'm choosing the black paint because my shoe is black." She describes details of her painting and also makes comments about her shoe. "Here is the sole of my shoe, and here are the laces. These dots are the holes where the laces go through the shoes. I really like these black shoes. I wear them to work and also to the grocery store, but I don't wear them to the park."

When she is finished painting, Ms. Jones tells the children that they will all have the opportunity to create a painting of their own shoes, either today or tomorrow, and that she will call them to the art center when it is their turn.

2. Ms. Jones dismisses children to centers.

3. During center time, Ms. Jones facilitates the small-group painting activity for groups of four children at a time. Each child has his or her own easel with a large piece of paper clipped to it.

The easels are next to the art shelf, which holds several prefilled jars of paint and a large collection of paintbrushes. As children begin the small-group activity, they choose paint containers and brushes and put them in the easel tray.

Table 2 (*continued*)

4. After gathering art supplies, each child removes one of his or her shoes and places it near the easel for easier viewing. Ms. Jones tells the children to begin painting pictures of their shoes, encouraging them to discuss their paintings as they create them. Ms. Jones uses prompts and questions to facilitate children's further descriptions and additional details. Here are some examples:

• What color are your shoes?

• Do you know what this part of your shoe is called?

• My shoe has laces, but it looks like your shoe fastens with Velcro.

• Where do you keep your shoes at home?

• Did someone help you put on your shoes this morning? Who helped?

• Where did you get those shoes? At the store, or maybe from a friend or family member?

5. As children are painting, Ms. Jones labels their pictures with the words and sentences they have used to describe their shoes. Ms. Jones also records children's dictations about their work in a notepad and takes a few photos of each child while he or she is working.

6 . When children are finished painting, they clean up their art supplies while Ms. Jones places their paintings on the drying rack.

Note. For more information about lesson planning and lesson planning resources, see the following resources: Grisham-Brown, Hemmeter, and Pretti-Frontczak (2005); LaRoque and Darling (2008).

come to the small group. Together, they identify potential barriers for some children to participate in the lesson and create strategies to overcome those barriers.

Ms. Jones first considers Joey, who has a developmental delay and Down syndrome. Joey often needs more support with academic tasks and self-help skills. Ms. Jones looks over her lesson and realizes that although Joey will enjoy the activity, he will probably become overwhelmed with the multiple questions and conversation starters she has planned to use as prompts. She knows that one of his IEP goals is that when involved in an activity, Joey will name the correct colors (red, blue, yellow) found in his environment (school, home, community) five out of five opportunities over 3 days. This goal is especially relevant because it expands Joey's expressive language skills and easily allows embedding within typical classroom activities and routines (Grisham-Brown & Hemmeter, 1998). Ms. Hernandez mentions that all other children in the class are also working on learning color words as part of the general curriculum. Ms. Jones decides that she will focus her conversation with Joey around the colors he chooses for his painting. In making this adaptation, Ms. Jones realizes that there are also a few young 3-year-olds in her classroom who might not be ready to discuss multiple topics while they are painting, and she makes a note to adapt the prompts in her lesson for Joey and for two other children. Although Joey sometimes has difficulty with self-help skills, he is very motivated by the art center and is competent in gathering his own art supplies and putting them away, so he will not need an adaptation for that aspect of the lesson.

Ms. Jones next considers Hailey, who has CP resulting in significant motor delays, especially on the left side of her body, and who uses a wheelchair for mobility. Hailey has strong verbal skills, and Ms. Jones does not feel that she will need to adapt her questions or prompts, but she may need to allow additional wait time for Hailey to respond. She makes a note of this on her lesson plan.

Ms. Jones's biggest concern for Hailey is making sure that the activity is physically accessible. First, she decides to clip Hailey's paper to the far right side of her easel, hoping this will give her the greatest access to it with her right hand. Next, she asks Ms. Hernandez to check the art center to make sure that (1) there is room for Hailey's wheelchair to fit between the easels and the art shelf and (2) the paints and paint brushes are placed near the front of the art shelf so Hailey can grab them with her right hand and put them on her wheelchair tray. Ms. Hernandez makes a few adjustments to the location of the easel and the art supplies, but she wants to be sure these adaptations are in place all the time, not just for this particular lesson, so she marks the chosen locations for the easel and art supplies with colored tape. Hailey's IEP includes a goal for her to become more independent in her classroom environment by choosing and setting up her own materials at center time; this activity addresses that goal. Ms. Jones jots down all of this information in her lesson plan.

Finally, Ms. Jones considers Aiden, a child without an IEP or diagnosed disability. He has trouble with wait times during small-group activities. Ms. Jones thinks about how she can make an adaptation that will reduce wait time for Aiden and remembers that his parents told her he is very motivated when completing simple chores. Ms. Jones decides that rather than wash paintbrushes or clean up small paint spills herself between groups, she will set out a small bucket of water and a sponge. She will ask Aiden to help with those jobs if he

is waiting for other children to arrive or finishes before the rest of the group. Ms. Jones realizes that a few other children can benefit from this adaptation as well and makes notes in her lesson plan.

Table 3 illustrates the changes that Ms. Jones made to her lesson plan as she adapted it for children with diverse learning needs. Notice the addition of a second column to the lesson planning form that focuses on addressing IEP goals and making adaptations.

It can be challenging to create an inclusive classroom environment in many types of settings, such as public preschool programs, Head Start classrooms, and child care centers. It can also be challenging to intentionally create lessons that address state standards, are meaningful and relevant, are developmentally appropriate, and are universal enough for all children, yet are adapted to meet the needs and learning goals of individual children, with and without disabilities. We recognize that teachers in different states and programs use a variety of planning tools and lesson plan formats. Readers are encouraged to focus on the processes discussed in this article, rather than on the specific forms that were provided, and to determine how those processes can be applied to their own planning forms and tools. Teachers interested in learning more about particular lesson planning strategies can consult Grisham-Brown et al. (2005) and LaRoque and Darling (2008).

Table 3
Revised Lesson Plan

Lesson plan	Embedded IEP goals/adaptations for individual children
Language Arts benchmark Children will describe familiar places, things, and events and, with teacher assistance, provide additional detail.	
Activity (10–12 minutes) Teacher will facilitate discussion and artistic representation of shoes during a small-group art activity. Conversation will focus on the children's shoes, on the location of shoes in their homes, and on how people help children put on and tie their shoes. Children will create paintings of their shoes as they talk.	
Materials (for all children) Child's own shoe, easel, paper, paint (variety of colors) in containers, and paintbrushes (variety of sizes)	Materials (for adaptations) Aiden: Sponge and bucket of water
Procedure 1. To introduce the small-group art activity, Ms. Jones models the lesson during large-group time. She removes one shoe, holds it up for the class, and describes it, saying "Here is my black shoe. It has laces. I get my shoes from my bedroom closet each morning. I put them on and tie them all by myself." (Before large-group time began, Ms. Jones placed an easel next to the large-group area, along with a few containers of paint and several paint brushes.) She now models the painting activity, narrating her actions as she works. She says, "I'm choosing the black paint because my shoe is black." She describes details of her painting and also makes comments about her shoe. "Here is the sole of my shoe, and here are the laces. These dots are the holes where the laces go through the shoes. I really like these black shoes. I wear them to work and also to the grocery store, but I don't wear them to the park."	IEP goal (Hailey): Facilitate independence in classroom environment by supporting Hailey in choosing and setting up materials at center time. Adaptation (Hailey): Place art supplies at the front of the art shelf. Clip paper to the right side of the easel.

Table 3 (continued)

When she is finished painting, Ms. Jones tells the children that they will all have the opportunity to create a painting of their own shoes, either today or tomorrow, and that she will call them to the art center when it is their turn.

2. Ms. Jones dismisses children to centers.

3. During center time, Ms. Jones facilitates the small-group painting activity for groups of four children at a time. Each child has his or her own easel with a large piece of paper clipped to it. The easels are next to the art shelf, which holds several prefilled jars of paint and a large collection of paintbrushes. As children begin the small-group activity, they choose paint containers and brushes and put them in the easel tray.

4. After gathering art supplies, each child removes one of his or her shoes and places it near the easel for easier viewing. Ms. Jones tells the children to begin painting pictures of their shoes, encouraging them to discuss their paintings as they create them. Ms. Jones uses prompts and questions to facilitate children's further descriptions and additional details. Here are some examples:
• What color are your shoes?
• Do you know what this part of your shoe is called?
• My shoe has laces, but it looks like your shoe fastens with Velcro.
• Where do you keep your shoes at your house?
• Did someone help you put on your shoes this morning? Who helped?
• Where did you get those shoes? At the store, or maybe from a friend or family member?

5. As children are painting, Ms. Jones labels their pictures with the words and sentences they have used to describe their shoes. Ms. Jones also records children's dictations about their work in a notepad and takes a few photos of each child while he or she is working.

6. When children are finished painting, they clean up their art supplies while Ms. Jones places their paintings on the drying rack.

Adaptation (Aiden/two other children): Provide a bucket of water and a sponge so children can clean up paint spills and wash paintbrushes to avoid wait time.

IEP goal (Joey): Focus conversation on color words (blue, red, yellow, green)

Adaptation (Joey and two other children): Reduce number of prompts and center conversation around color words.

Adaptation (Hailey): Allow additional wait time for Hailey to respond.

Note. See Sandall and Schwartz (2008) for information about adapting lesson plans. IEP = individualized education plan.

Conclusion

After implementing the small group art lesson to address her state's language arts benchmark, Ms. Jones sits down with Ms. Hernandez to debrief about the experience.

Ms. Jones feels proud that she was able to apply the principles of DAP in meeting the needs of all children while also incorporating specialized instruction for individual students. Also, due to her careful planning, Ms. Jones did not struggle to make the activity accessible to children as they worked and thus was able to better document progress using dictations and photographs.

Ms. Jones and Ms. Hernandez decide to dedicate a portion of their planning time each week to reviewing lesson plans for needed adaptations. They are excited about their new resources and strategies and want to share their skills with the rest of the staff. Ms. Jones makes arrangements with the school principal to lead a small workshop about lesson planning adaptations at the next professional development day.

When teachers of young children intentionally plan classroom projects and design lesson plans that align with state early learning standards, they address the full range of content areas (e.g., language arts, mathematics, social/emotional well-being, fine arts, science, social studies, and motor skills) important for young children's growth and development. Adapting the classroom environment, project work, and individual lessons to developmentally and individually meet the needs of *all* children's learning goals requires intentional planning and reflection on the part of the teacher (see Table 1). It is important to follow a systematic process for thinking about how lesson plans can address early learning standards (see Table 2) while targeting each child's meaningful participation and addressing supports to meet IEP or other individual learning goals (see Table 3). Additionally, teachers of young children may want to take advantage of the many resources available to them to assist with adapting routines and activities for a young child with disabilities. These resources may include collaborative planning meetings with the child's parents (either in person,

Adapting the classroom environment, project work, and individual lessons to developmentally and individually meet the needs of all children's learning goals requires intentional planning and reflection on the part of the teacher.

Table 4

Resources to Address the Needs of Diverse Learners in Early Care and Education Settings

Title, author, year	Description, Web site (if available)
Early Childhood Inclusion: A Joint Position Statement of the Division for Early Childhood (DEC) and the National Association for the Education of Young Children (NAEYC) DEC/NAEYC (2009)	This short paper outlines the key principles of inclusion in early childhood environments. http://www.naeyc.org/files/naeyc/file/positions/DEC_NAEYC_EC_updatedKS.pdf
Basics of Developmentally Appropriate Practices: An Introduction for Teachers of Children 3 to 6 Carol Copple & Sue Bredekamp (2006)	This little book describes the core concepts of developmentally appropriate practices and makes them meaningful for everyday practice for preschool teachers.
Building Blocks for Teaching Preschoolers With Special Needs Edited by Susan Sandall & Ilene Schwartz (2008)	A guide for preschool teachers to implement practical, research-based inclusion strategies that promote progress in critical areas such as behavior, emergent literacy, and peer relationships so they can more fully include children with disabilities in their classrooms.
CARA's Kit Suzanne A. Milbourne & Philippa Campbell (2007)	A flip-book that provides guidance for making adaptations to daily activities and routines so children ages 3 to 6 with disabilities and other special needs can successfully participate in all classroom activities.
"How Do You Individualize? Three Strategies for Supporting Every Learner" Lauren Baker (2014)	An article from *Teaching Young Children* focused on basic individualization strategies that preschool teachers can use every day. http://www.naeyc.org/tyc/infographic/how-do-you-individualize

with phone calls, or through e-mail) and with professional colleagues familiar with the child's learning needs. Teachers can participate in online and face-to-face professional development opportunities to learn more about current and new recommended practices in the field (Sheridan, Edwards, Marvin, & Knoche, 2009). Fortunately, early childhood teachers today can refer to books and journal articles that describe evidence-based strategies for supporting each child in order to ensure the meaningful participation of all young learners in the early childhood classroom. (See Table 4 for resources that highlight key ideas presented in this article.)

Creating a high-quality, inclusive early childhood classroom is a complex process. Teachers may need to rely on a variety of resources to support this process. Ms. Jones, the teacher in our vignette, intentionally provides all of the children with meaningful learning experiences that align with state early learning standards. Additionally, she is able to adapt instruction and document progress on a range of individual children's goals. Teachers of young children in inclusive settings cannot accomplish all of these tasks by working in isolation but must have the support of administrators, parents, and colleagues to carry out the vision of a truly inclusive early learning community.

Note

For more information, please contact Emily Dorsey at edorsey@illinois.edu

Preparation of this manuscript was supported, in part, by a leadership grant from the Office of Special Education Programs (Project BLEND, H325D110037) and a grant from the Illinois State Board of Education for the Illinois Early Learning Project at the University of Illinois at Urbana-Champaign (D6548). Opinions reflect those of the authors and do not necessarily reflect those of the granting agencies

References

Baker, L. (2014). How do you individualize? Three strategies for supporting every learner. *Teaching Young Children, 7*(2) 12-13. Retrieved July 15, 2014, from http://www.naeyc.org/tyc/infographic/how-do-you-individualize

Beneke, S. J. & Ostrosky, M. M. (2013). The potential of the project approach to support diverse young learners. *Young Children, 68*(2), 22-28.

Copple, C. & Bredekamp, S. (2006). *Basics of developmentally appropriate practice: An introduction for teachers of children 3 to 6.* Washington, DC: National Association for the Education of Young Children.

Division for Early Childhood/National Association for the Education of Young Children (DEC/NAEYC). (2009, April). *Early childhood inclusion: A joint position statement of the Division for Early Childhood (DEC) and the National Association for the Education of Young Children (NAEYC).* Chapel Hill, NC: The University of North Carolina, FPG Child Development Institute. Retrieved Month Day, Year, from http://npdci.fpg.unc.edu/resources/articles/Early_Childhood_Inclusion/

Gebhard, B. (2010, November). *Putting standards into practice: States' use of early learning guidelines for infants and toddlers.* Retrieved July 15, 2014, from the Zero to Three website: http://www.zeroto-three.org/public-policy/webinars-conference-calls/states-use-of-elg-for-it-final.pdf

Grisham-Brown, J., Hemmeter, M. L., & Pretti-Frontczak, K. (2005). *Blended practices for teaching young children in inclusive settings.* Baltimore, MD: Brookes.

Illinois State Board of Education. (2013, September). *Illinois early learning and development standards, preschool.* Springfield, IL: Author. Retrieved July 14, 2014, from http://illinoisearlylearning.org/ields/ields.pdf

Individuals With Disabilities Education Act, 20 U.S.C. § 1400 (2004).

Katz, L. (2014). Standards of experience. *Teaching Young Children, 7*(3), 6-7.

LaRoque, M. & Darling, S. M. (2008). *Blended curriculum in the inclusive K-3 classroom: Teaching all young children.* Boston, MA: Pearson.

Milbourne, S. A. & Campbell, P. H. (2007). *CARA's kit. Creating adaptations for routines and activities.* Philadelphia, PA: Thomas Jefferson University, Research Institute, Child and Family Studies.

National Association for the Education of Young Children (NAEYC). (2009). *Developmentally appropriate practice in early childhood programs serving children from birth through age 8.* Washington, DC: Author. Retrieved July 15, 2014, from https://www.naeyc.org/files/naeyc/file/positions/PSDAP.pdf

National Association for the Education of Young Children (NAEYC) & National Association of Early Childhood Specialists in State Departments of Education. (2009). *Where we stand on early learning standards.* Washington, DC: Authors. Retrieved July 15, 2014, from http://www.naeyc.org/positionstate-ments/learning_standards

National Center on Child Care Quality Improvement. (2013, January). *State/territory early learning guidelines.* Fairfax, VA: Author. Retrieved July 15, 2014, from https://childcareta.acf.hhs.gov/sites/default/files/075_1301_state_elgs_web_0.pdf

Odom, S. L., Buysse, V., & Soukakou, E. (2011). Inclusion for young children with disabilities: A quarter century of research perspectives. *Journal of Early Intervention, 33*, 344–356. doi:10.1177/1053815111430094

Sandall, S. Hemmeter, M. L., Smith, B. J., & McLean, M. E. (2005). *DEC recommended practices: A comprehensive guide for practical applications in early intervention/early childhood special education.* Longmont, CO: Sopris West.

Sandall, S. R. & Schwartz, I. S. (2008). *Building blocks for teaching preschoolers with special needs* (2nd ed.). Baltimore, MD: Brookes.

Schwartz, I. S., Sandall, S. R., Odom, S. L., Horn, E., & Beckman, P. J. (2002). "I know it when I see it": In search of a common definition of inclusion. In S. L. Odom (Ed.), *Widening the circle: Including children with disabilities in preschool programs* (pp. 10–24). New York, NY: Teachers College Press.

Scott-Little, C., Lesko, J., Martella, J., & Milburn, P. (2007). Early learning standards: Results from a national survey to document trends in state-level policies and practices. *Early Childhood Research and Practice, 9*(1). Retrieved July 15, 2014, from http://ecrp.illinois.edu/v9n1/little.html

Sheridan, S. M., Edwards, C. P., Marvin, C. A., & Knoche, L.L. (2009). Professional development in early childhood programs: Process issues and research needs. *Early Education and Development, 20*, 377-401. doi:10.1080/10409280802582795

U.S. Department of Education, Office of Special Education and Rehabilitative Services. (2012, February). *OSEP Dear colleague letter on preschool (LRE).* Washington, DC: Author. Retrieved July 15, 2014, from https://www2.ed.gov/policy/speced/guid/idea/memosdcltrs/preschoollre22912.pdf

Winton, P. J., McCollum, J. A., & Catlett, C. (Eds.). (2008). *Practical approaches to early childhood professional development: Evidence, strategies, and resources.* Washington, DC: Zero to Three.

Yell, M. L. (2006). *The law and special education* (2nd ed.). Upper Saddle River, NJ: Pearson.

Blending Practices to Support Early Childhood Inclusion

A Step-by-Step Process to Guide Itinerant Early Childhood Special Education Services

Laurie A. Dinnebeil, Ph.D.,

William F. McInerney, Ph.D.
University of Toledo

After 10 years of providing classroom-based instruction to preschool-aged children with special needs, Amanda is starting a new job as an itinerant early childhood special education (ECSE) teacher. Although she's excited about her new role, she's not sure where to begin. She knew the routine in preschool, but she is not so sure how to spend her time when she travels to early childhood education (ECE) programs. The very first child she is visiting is Riley, a little boy with a language delay. Riley has limited expressive language skills and is having difficulty interacting with the other children in the classroom. How can Amanda best help children like Riley? How can she help Riley's ECE teacher, Shelly, be successful and feel comfortable and confident? What should she focus on in preparing for visits or during visits? How can she best spend her time? Here is a process for Amanda to learn her role . . . step by step!

Odom et al. (1999) defined two primary types of itinerant service delivery in early childhood special education (ECSE). One model involves the itinerant ECSE (IECSE) teacher providing direct services to the child, usually one-on-one or in small groups with typically developing peers. A second model requires the IECSE teacher to serve primarily as a consultant. The IECSE teacher helps the child's general early childhood education (ECE) teacher, caregiver, or parent provide individualized intervention that is embedded in the child's daily routines and activities (Dinnebeil & McInerney, 2011). This *consultative* approach to IECSE service delivery helps general ECE teachers find ways to address children's individualized education program (IEP) goals and objectives during daily and weekly routines via an embedded IEP-focused intervention. The adoption of a consultative approach is a recommended practice in ECSE (Horn, Lieber, Li, Sandall, & Schwartz, 2000; Wolery, 2005). The purpose of this paper is to provide an overview of how IECSE teachers can use the practices described to provide high-quality services to young children with disabilities enrolled in community-based early childhood programs.[1]

If the role of the IECSE teacher is to effectively support early childhood inclusion, what should itinerant teachers like Amanda do during their regular visits to early childhood classrooms? It is difficult to find evidence to suggest that a direct service approach, in which the itinerant teacher interacts with Riley to help him reach his developmental or academic goals, works. Whereas this sort of "tutoring" approach might work for older students, particularly in addressing specific academic content, young children like Riley usually lack the ability to regulate their behavior or attention in order to benefit from episodic interventions (Bowman, Donovan, & Burns, 2000; Shonkoff & Phillips, 2000). There is, however, a substantial research base that supports the use of embedded or naturalistic interventions with preschool-aged children like Riley (Pretti-Frontczak & Bricker, 2001; Sandall & Schwartz, 2008). Yet, adoption of an embedded intervention model is just one step in a process that supports successful early childhood inclusion. Before that can happen, IECSE teachers like Amanda need to consider other intervention practices that help to set the stage for successfully embedding intervention. Our work with IECSE teachers and their supervisors, as well as the adults with whom they partner (i.e., general ECE teachers, parents, or other caregivers), has

> *This* consultative *approach to* IECSE service delivery helps general ECE teachers find ways to address children's individualized education plan (IEP) goals and objectives during daily and weekly routines via an embedded IEP-focused intervention.

---

[1] For the purposes of this paper, we focus on IECSE services provided in early childhood classrooms. However, IECSE teachers who provide services to young children in their homes can apply the same steps outlined in this paper, working with the parent or caregiver in place of the ECE partner teacher.

led us to develop a nine-step model of blended intervention practices that may be a useful guide for IECSE teachers and those with whom they work. This IECSE service delivery model describes an evidence-based approach to early childhood intervention in community-based settings. Each of the nine steps in the process is briefly described. The overview is intended to lead to a better understanding of how each of the practices can work together to support effective early childhood intervention.

Step 1: Identify Functional IEP Goals and Objectives

The IEP provides the blueprint for services for young children with disabilities. The most important components of the IEP are the goals and objectives that identify important competencies associated with success in the current and next environments. Determining the focus of intervention is the primary purpose of IEP planning. The IEP, therefore, must be developed to enhance functional outcomes of IEP goals and objectives (Jung, 2007; McWilliam & Casey, 2008).

Jung (2007) outlined five criteria for determining the "functionality" of IEP objectives by using the acronym SMART and included the following criteria:

1. *Specific?* Does the IEP objective address specific knowledge and skills? That is, do all members of the IEP team share a common understanding of the desired outcome?
2. *Measurable?* Is the IEP objective written so that the team can measure the child's progress?
3. *Attainable?* Effective IEP objectives are those that the child can attain in 2 to 4 months.
4. *Routines-based?* The ability to generalize newly acquired skills or information to other settings or situations increases when children learn these skills in context. For young children, context refers to the daily routines or activities that compose their days. Team members should be able to address IEP objectives within the context of the child's daily routines, wherever they occur.
5. *Tied to a functional priority?* Effective IEP objectives are those that reflect learning priorities that team members have identified for the child. For example, using a pincer grasp is a functional skill; however, picking up raisins from a smooth surface, in isolation from other relevant grasping tasks or outside of the context of snack time or housekeeping play, is not.

Step 2: Confirm the "Goodness of Fit" Between the Learning Environment and the Child's Needs and Make Adjustments as Needed

Access, participation, and support are defining features of early childhood inclusion (Division for Early Childhood [DEC]/National Association for the Education of Young Children [NAEYC], 2009). In high-quality programs, young children can access a broad range of learning activities and opportunities; having a disability should not limit or prohibit that access. Participation, with respect to inclusion, describes the extent to which young children with special needs have meaningful opportunities to be engaged in classroom activities and routines. This may require providing appropriate supports to young children so they are successful. This also may necessitate providing support to those adults who work with the child. An important task of an IECSE teacher like Amanda is to ensure that the learning environment matches the child's needs. The IECSE teacher must work with the ECE partner teacher to ensure a goodness of fit between the child's capabilities, needs, and interests and the learning environment. IECSE teachers like Amanda and their general ECE partner teachers like Shelly should consider the principles of universal design for learning (Nolet & McLaughlin, 2000), which address the development and selection of learning materials and adaptations of the learning environment in an effort to be responsive to the needs of all children, when evaluating the extent to which the learning environment supports the needs of the child.

Amanda and Shelly can also evaluate the quality of the environment using a scale such as the Inclusive Classroom Profile (Soukakou, 2012). The Inclusive Classroom Profile is a rating scale that uses rubrics for observation to determine the extent or degree of inclusive practices and child engagement that are apparent in an ostensibly inclusive setting. Use of such a scale can be helpful in determining whether modifications of the classroom environment, toys and learning materials, the daily schedule, routines, and/or instructional approaches would support learning. Using a rating scale can provide the structure to conduct a comprehensive observation, ensuring that teachers do not overlook important components of the learning environment.

Once Amanda and Shelly have evaluated the learning environment, they can use tools such as CARA's Kit (Milbourne & Campbell, 2007) and CARA's Checklist of Priorities and Concerns that is included in CARA's Kit to guide adaptations or modifications that will support children's access to the curriculum and their participation in all learning activities. CARA's Kit provides concrete examples of how to transform IEP objectives into embedded learning opportunities that are responsive to transdisciplinary intervention in inclusive environments. One of the things that Amanda and Shelly found was that they could modify the learning environment in order to create more motivating opportunities for Riley to use language when requesting objects from his peers.

Step 3: Prioritize IEP Objectives

IEP objectives can be intimidating to general ECE teachers like Shelly who have limited knowledge or expertise in early childhood intervention. Also, because IECSE teachers and their ECE partner teachers often have limited time to work together, it is helpful to have an effective strategy for determining the most efficient use of that time. Without such a strategy, it is difficult to determine where to begin the intervention process. Do you start with the first objective on the IEP and work down the list? Start with the easiest objective and leave the most difficult for last? In this article, we describe two different approaches that one could use to prioritize IEP objectives. Each approach is useful; readers can decide which of the two strategies to use. The important point here is to take the time to review IEP objectives and use a systematic approach to prioritizing work on IEP objectives.

Wolery, Brashers, and Nietzel (2002) described an ecological congruence approach that enables IECSE teachers and their ECE partner teachers to identify preschool activities and routines that present the greatest challenges to young children with disabilities and their teachers. They developed an observational assessment to identify challenging routines and activities and used the results of the assessment to prioritize skills, behaviors, or knowledge that were critical to successful participation. For example, Riley struggles with interacting with his peers. Instead of asking for toys or materials, Riley might engage in aggressive behaviors such as grabbing, pinching, or hitting other children. It would be important for the Amanda and Shelly to help Riley learn more appropriate ways to request objects because that would help him to interact more appropriately with his peers as well as increase his expressive language skills. In this case, Riley's IEP objectives related to these skills would be addressed first.

...because IECSE teachers and their ECE partner teachers often have limited time to work together, it is helpful to have an effective strategy for determining the most efficient use of that time.

We also have developed a strategy for prioritizing IEP-based instruction based on the salient characteristics of the target skill or behavior the IEP objective addresses. This process of vetting the IEP could be offset if the ECE partner teacher was actively engaged in the development of the IEP and also was a participant in the IEP meeting. Although this engagement of ECE partner teachers is clearly recommended in the Individuals With Disabilities Education Act (IDEA; 2004), this is a work in progress. Certainly there are a number of ECE partner teachers in community programs who, unfortunately, are not actively involved in the process of IEP development and do not participate in the IEP meeting, either personally or via any remote-access technology. In accord with the mandates of IDEA, we recommend proactive involvement of all key constituents in the IEP process; specifically, we endorse full participation by lead ECE teachers when the child in question will receive IEP-focused services in a community preschool or child care program. As long as opportunity for participation in the IEP process and the IEP meeting is not guaranteed by current local education agency practices, we recommend a critical review of the IEP by the IECSE and ECE partner teachers. In some cases (e.g., child transitions from one program to the next), it may be that the child's general ECE teacher or even the IECSE teacher has not been part of the IEP team. If this is the case, it becomes even more important to jointly review the IEP goals and objectives so there is a common understanding of the goals for instruction.

The following four categories describe the maturation, environment, peer-interaction, and intensive/direct instruction (MEPI) process and factors inherent in intervention or instruction that could effectively support acquisition of a skill or behavior:

1. *Maturation*: Evaluate the IEP objective to see whether the target behavior or skill is likely to improve as a result of biological development and interaction with environmental experiences, without significant teacher or peer involvement. The presumption concerning maturation is that there will be many naturally occurring opportunities during the day that will allow the child opportunity for practice and refinement. The relevant judgment of the IEP team, or IECSE/ECE teacher dyad, is that unplanned and naturally occurring opportunities will be sufficient to support the development of the targeted skill/behavior in a high-quality, inclusive early childhood learning environment.

2. *Environment*: Evaluate the IEP objective to see whether the target behavior or skill is likely to improve as a result of child having

access to learning materials that facilitate this skill/behavior or intentional arrangement of the learning environment to elicit this skill/behavior.

3. *Peer Interaction*: Evaluate the learning objective to see whether the target behavior or skill is likely to improve as a result of casual and/or intentional interaction with competent peer models.

4. *Intensive/Direct Intervention*: Evaluate the learning objective to see whether the target behavior or skill is an immediate concern (e.g., aggressive behavior, expected skills in next environment, would improve social valence) and whether the child would not be expected to make reasonable progress in acquiring this skill/behavior without direct and consistent use of a child-focused intervention.

Using the approach described above, IECSE teachers and their ECE partner teachers would focus most of their attention on those objectives categorized as needing direct or intensive intervention. It should be clear that the categories of developmental support described in the MEPI model are not mutually exclusive and are dependent upon the age and developmental characteristics of the child. If they had completed Step 2 of the MEPI process correctly (analyzing the learning environment), modifications or adaptations that would address IEP objectives would be categorized as maturation or environment. It is important to note that whereas the child's progress toward mastering these objectives would be monitored, the IECSE or ECE partner teacher would not provide direct intervention unless necessary, as indicated by failure of the child to develop the target skill/behavior or by an increase in the intensity or frequency of an undesirable behavior. The category of peer interaction is similar to maturation and environment in the assumption that the child will progress if there are opportunities to interact with more competent peers. Under the peer interaction category, the IECSE teacher and the ECE partner teacher may initiate evidence-based, peer-mediated intervention strategies that could be expected to support children's progress without direct intervention from the teacher.

It is important that teachers monitor the child's progress toward meeting all IEP objectives regardless of their designation as amenable to support via any of the MEPI factors. We also recommend that the IEP team reconsider placement options if the results of the MEPI analysis indicate that all or most of the child's IEP objectives must be addressed via direct intervention. If that is the case, perhaps a "regular" ECE program (i.e., a program characterized by enrollment of few children with special needs or a history of enrolling only children with more mild forms of developmental delay) is not the most appropriate setting for the provision of special education services for the child in question.

Step 4: Identify Embedded Learning Opportunities

Once the IECSE teacher and the ECE partner teachers have identified high-priority IEP objectives, they need to analyze the classroom schedule to determine the routines and activities during which the child is likely to need to exhibit the target skill or behavior. For example, consider Riley's difficulty using language when requesting objects from peers. Amanda and Shelly may decide that center time and snack time are routines that would provide Riley with multiple opportunities to practice appropriately requesting objects from peers (toys and materials during center time, food and juice during snack). Amanda and Shelly can use curriculum-planning matrices, like those developed by Grisham-Brown, Hemmeter, and Pretti-Frontczak (2005) or Pretti-Frontczak and Bricker (2004), to identify opportunities. Daily activities are listed across the top of the matrix and the child's IEP objectives are listed in the left-hand column. Activities that provide naturally occurring opportunities for learning a skill or behavior are identified on the matrix with a brief description of how the teacher(s) could address the objective. For example, Amanda and Shelly may note "Prompt Riley to request items from peers at different centers (e.g., crayons at the Art Area, blocks at the Block Area)" in the corresponding box on the matrix. A planning matrix will help to identify opportunities during the day when the ECE partner teacher can address IEP objectives. Table 1 provides readers with a snapshot from Riley's curriculum matrix.

It is important that teachers monitor the child's progress toward meeting all IEP objectives regardless of their designation as amenable to support via the maturation, environment, peer-interaction, and intensive/direct instruction (MEPI) process.

General Considerations When Using a Planning Matrix. We strongly encourage IECSE teachers and ECE partner teachers to complete the planning matrix together. Although it might seem more efficient for IECSE teachers to complete the matrix and share it with their ECE partner teachers, we believe that a collaborative approach has many benefits.

Table 1
A Snapshot From Riley's Curriculum Matrix

IEP objective	Arrival	Circle time	Center time	Snack	Outdoors	Small group
Use language to request items from peers			Prompt Riley to request items from peers at different centers (e.g., crayons at the Art Area, blocks at the Block Area)	~~Prompt Riley to request more to drink or eat from peers~~	Prompt Riley to request use of bicycle or other outdoor items	Add opportunities to prompt Riley to request items from his peers during small-group activities
			Gain Riley's attention		Gain Riley's attention	Gain Riley's attention
			Present the controlling prompt		Present the controlling prompt	Present the controlling prompt
			Wait for Riley to respond		Wait for Riley to respond	Wait for Riley to respond
			Provide appropriate feedback or reinforcement		Provide appropriate feedback or reinforcement	Provide appropriate feedback or reinforcement

Note. "Prompt Riley to request more to drink or eat from peers" is deleted because Amanda's partner ECE teacher felt as if she could not realistically offer Riley that learning opportunity during snack.

In addition to the positive benefits for the partnership, a collaborative approach can allay the concerns of ECE partner teachers about learning a new tool as well as provide a scaffold for an adult learner to master the skill of matrix planning. When IECSE teachers make decisions unilaterally, they may not be aware of other factors that affect the degree to which expectations for embedding interventions are realistic. For example, although snack time might appear to be an ideal time to help Riley learn to request objects from peers using language, when working in isolation, Amanda might not know that Shelly's classroom assistant takes her break during this time and that Shelly must assume sole responsibility for monitoring all the children. See Table 1 for how a learning opportunity was removed from the matrix after Amanda and Shelly discussed the daily routine. On the other hand, if they work together, Shelly might identify other activities or routines that offer more realistic routines or activities (e.g., small group time). See Table 1 for a learning opportunity that was added to the matrix after Amanda and Shelly discussed the daily routine. IECSE teachers can become much more aware of the rhythms and routines of the child's classroom when they plan collaboratively with ECE partner teachers.

Step 5: Identify Appropriate Teaching Strategies

Amanda and Shelly identified two activities in which they could embed instruction that supported Riley's ability to request objects from peers: center time and outside time. Their next step is to determine the type of intervention strategy that they will use to support Riley. Amanda and Shelly should consider using evidence-based intervention strategies that the partner teacher can easily implement during a specific activity (Buysse, Wesley, Snyder, & Winton, 2006). Fortunately there are a variety of digital and print resources that describe evidence-based child-focused intervention strategies. For example, the Autism Internet Modules (AIM) available through the Ohio Center for Autism and Low Incidence Disabilities (www.ocali.org) provide a comprehensive repository of evidence-based intervention strategies that are appropriate to use with young children who have special learning needs, including those with autism spectrum disorder. These modules also include overviews of procedural components and procedural implementation checklists that IECSE teachers can share with others. We also encourage IECSE teachers like Amanda to identify child-focused intervention strategies that are consistent with DEC Recommended Practices (Division of Early Childhood, 2014).

Step 6: Determine a Progress Monitoring Strategy

It is important to identify a progress monitoring strategy that is efficient and yields valid and reliable information about the effectiveness of the intervention (DEC, 2007; Greenwood et al., 2011; Raver, 2003, 2004). Determining an appropriate progress monitoring strategy is dependent upon the nature of the IEP objective as addressed in Steps 1 and 3 as well as on the specific, child-focused intervention strategy chosen in Step 5. In the example above, Amanda and Shelly agreed to encourage Riley to ask for objects from peers during center and outside times using a time-delay strategy (Doyle, Wolery, Gast, Ault, & Wiley, 1990). Their next step is to jointly identify child progress monitoring strategies that can be easily implemented during these routines. There is a range of valid and reliable data collection strategies, including frequency counts, level of assistance recording, interval sampling, permanent products, and duration record-ing. As they decide on a progress monitoring strategy, it is important for them to reach agreement on what constitutes a correct response for Riley as well as a consistent process for recording behavior.

For IECSE services to work effectively, ECE teachers, parents, or other caregivers must assume some responsibility for monitoring and data col-lection. If these individuals are the ones who will use the progress moni-toring strategy, then they must be able to use it within the context of their busy routines. For this reason, designing the data collection plan must be a joint effort. Jointly collecting data during some practice sessions and discussing the data collection process is time well spent if IECSE teach-ers and their partners have access to valid and reliable information to make instructional decisions that support children's progress. After some discussion of the benefits and drawbacks of different progress monitor-ing strategies, Amanda and Shelly agreed that the best way to monitor Riley's progress was to document the amount of help that Riley needed to request objects from peers. Amanda developed data collection sheets appropriate for collecting this information and she, along with Shelly, tried them out to make sure that they were easy for Shelly to use given her other responsibilities.

Step 7: Coaching to Help Other Adults Effectively Use the Intervention Strategy

Implementation research suggests that coaching is one of the most effec-tive ways of helping practitioners to transfer research knowledge to prac-tice (Fixsen, Blasé, Timbers, & Wolf, 2007). Coaching can help others build and refine the skills necessary to effectively address the needs of young children with disabilities (Fox, Hemmeter, Snyder, Binder, & Clarke, 2011). Providing a detailed description of the coaching process is beyond the scope of this paper. However, we do identify tools that might be helpful to use when coaching a learner (i.e., an ECE partner teacher or other adult) on how to use a child-focused intervention strategy.

It is important that both the coach and the learner have a clear understanding of the strategy they identified in Step 5. This includes identifying the procedural components of a particular skill or strategy, as well as the order in which these components should be implemented. For example, Amanda and Shelly decided to use time delay (Doyle et al., 1990) as the way they would support Riley in requesting objects from peers. In order to use time delay, Shelly needed to learn how to gain the Riley's attention, present the controlling prompt, wait for Riley to respond, and then provide appropriate feedback or reinforcement.

...designing the data collection plan must be a joint effort.

One way that IECSE teachers can coach their partners is through the use of implementation checklists (Dinnebeil, Spino, & McInerney, 2011). An implementation checklist outlines the required components of an intervention strategy in the sequence in which these components should occur. The checklist serves as a reminder of the steps and sequence in this procedure for those who will be implementing the intervention strategy during the IECSE teacher's absence. The AIM Modules (available through the Ohio Center for Autism and Low Incidence at www.ocali.org) contain a comprehensive inventory of implementation checklists. We encourage IECSE teachers to access this valuable resource, but we caution them to be sure that the terminology used in the checklist is easy to understand for someone without a special education background or a partner with limited literacy skills. In the case of Riley's teachers, Amanda developed an implementation checklist focused on how to use time delay (Doyle et al., 1990) to help Riley request objects from his peers during center time and outdoor time. Amanda used the checklist to coach Shelly on how to implement the time-delay strategy during center time and outside time.

Using an implementation checklist involves a series of steps (Dinnebeil et al., 2011). First, the coach (i.e., Amanda) and the learner (i.e., Shelly) should review the implementation checklist to make sure that each of them understands the terminology. Second, the coach demonstrates the use of the strategy to the learner, having the learner use the implementation checklist as a guide. The learner provides feedback to the coach about the coach's level of implementation. Third, the learner demonstrates the use of the strategy, and the coach uses the implementation checklist as a guide to provide feedback. This cycle of modeling and providing feedback continues until the learner states or demonstrates that he or she can competently use the strategy in the IECSE teacher's absence.

Step 8: Monitor Use of the Teaching Strategy

After Shelly has learned the steps involved in using time delay, she needs to incorporate the strategy into daily routines and activities identified in Step 4 of the process. At this point, Amanda's role is to step back and provide the ongoing support that Shelly needs in order to use the strategy and monitor its effectiveness. In order to determine whether the child-focused intervention strategy identified in Step 5 is effective, it is helpful to document when and if the strategy has been implemented with fidelity (i.e., follows the steps outlined in the implementation checklist in sequence). The ECE teacher can also use the implementation checklist to document that he or she has implemented the strategy with fidelity. This record can be helpful in the next step of the process: evaluating the effectiveness of the time-delay strategy embedded into the intervention strategy. It is at this stage that Shelly also incorporates the child-focused progress-monitoring strategy, described in Step 6.

Delivering high quality itinerant ECSE services is a complex process that involves the effective use of a range of evidence-based practices.

Step 9: Evaluate the Success of the Process

After completing Steps 1–8, Amanda and Shelly should have collected data on the child's progress, as well as data that describe how well and how often Shelly is implementing time delay. Data from both sources are necessary to determine whether the intervention they have agreed upon (embedding the use of time delay in center- and outdoor-time activities) and have implemented is working or whether they need to revise it. Before they can determine whether the strategy is effective, both must agree that Shelly has implemented the intervention strategies with fidelity. Teachers, parents, and caregivers have multiple responsibilities during the child's day. It is entirely conceivable that they might find, after the fact, that the expectation to implement a certain strategy was unrealistic. For example, implementing a strategy such as time delay during outside time may have proved to be too difficult because Shelly had other responsibilities at this time that she overlooked. If fidelity data suggest this, then it is important that Amanda and Shelly discuss the situation objectively and revise the intervention plan. The intent of this discussion is not to make Shelly feel guilty for not following through with the plan, but rather to revise the intervention plan so they can adopt effective strategies to replace the ineffective strategies. If it becomes apparent that the ECE partner teacher (for whatever reasons) has not implemented the intervention strategies as planned, across a number of IEP objectives or across children in the classroom, the child's IEP team might reconsider the decision to provide itinerant services. If the interventions do appear to be working, the team or IECSE teacher should either continue or fade the intervention while documenting the child's progress and addressing other IEP goals and objectives, as appropriate.

Conclusion

Amanda was unsure about what she should do as an IECSE teacher. We believe that using the process we have outlined in this paper can help itinerant teachers like Amanda (as well as other ECSE teachers) use her time effectively and expeditiously to support children and the adults who work with them on a regular basis. Delivering high-quality itinerant ECSE services is a complex process that involves the effective use of a range of evidence-based practices. Each of the nine steps in the process, as outlined in this paper, rests on an evidence base that has guided the field of early childhood intervention. We believe that this process IECSE service delivery can effectively support children's developmental and academic progress in inclusive early childhood programs . . . step by step!

Note

For more information, please contact Laurie A. Dinnebeil at laurie.dinnebeil@utoledo.edu

References

Bowman, B., Donovan, M. S., & Burns, M. S. (2000). *Eager to learn: Educating our preschoolers.* Washington, DC: National Academies Press.

Buysse, V., Wesley, P. W., Snyder, P., & Winton, P. (2006). Evidence-based practices: What does it really mean for the early childhood field? *Young Exceptional Children, 9,* 2-11.

Dinnebeil, L. A. & McInerney, W. F. (2011). *A guide to itinerant ECSE service delivery.* Baltimore: Brookes Publishing.

Dinnebeil, L. A., Spino, M., & McInerney, W. F. (2011). Using implementation checklists to reinforce the use of child-focused intervention strategies. *Young Exceptional Children, 14*(2), 22-31.

Division for Early Childhood (DEC). (2007). *Promoting positive outcomes for children with disabilities: Recommendations for curriculum, assessment, and program evaluation.* Missoula, MT: Author.

Division for Early Childhood (DEC)/National Association for the Education of Young Children (NAEYC). (2009). *Early childhood inclusion: A position statement of the Division for Early Childhood (DEC) and the National Association for the Education of Young Children (NAEYC).* Chapel Hill, NC: The University of North Carolina, FPG Child Development Institute.

Doyle, P. M, Wolery, M., Gast, D. L., Ault, M. J., & Wiley, K. (1990). Comparison of constant time delay and the system of least prompts in teaching preschoolers with developmental delays. *Research in Developmental Disabilities, 11,* 1-22.

Fixsen, D. L., Blasé, K. A., Timbers, G. D., & Wolf, M. M. (2007). In search of program implementation: 792 replications of the Teaching-Family model. *Behavior Analyst Today, 8,* 96-110.

Fox, L., Hemmeter, M. L., Snyder, P., Binder, D. P., & Clarke, S. (2011). Coaching early childhood special educators to implement a comprehensive model for promoting young children's social competence. *Topics in Early Childhood Special Education, 31,* 178-192.

Grisham-Brown, J., Hemmeter, M. L., & Pretti-Frontczak, K. (2005). *Blended practices for teaching young children in inclusive settings.* Baltimore, MD: Brookes.

Grisham-Brown, J., Pretti-Frontczak, K., Hemmeter, M.L., & Ridgley, R. (2002). Teaching IEP goals and objectives in the context of classroom routines and activities. *Young Exceptional Children, 6,* 18-27.

Horn, E., Lieber, J., Li, S., Sandall, S., & Schwartz, I. (2000). Supporting young children's IEP goals in inclusive settings through embedded learning opportunities. *Topics in Early Childhood Special Education, 20*(4), 208–223.

Jung, L. A. (2007). Writing SMART objectives and strategies that fit the routine. *Young Exceptional Children, 39,* 54–58.

McWilliam, R. A. & Casey, A. M. (2008). *Engagement of every child in the preschool classroom.* Baltimore: Brookes.

Milbourne, S. A. & Campbell, P. H. (2007). *CARA's Kit: Creating adaptations for routines and activities.* Washington, DC: Council for Exceptional Children.

Nolet, V. & McLaughlin, M. J. (2000). *Accessing the general curriculum: Including students with disabilities in standards-based reform.* Thousand Oaks, CA: Corwin Press.

Odom, S. L., Horn, E., Marquart, J. M., Hanson, M. J., Wolfberg, P., Beckman, P., et al. (1999). On the forms of inclusion: Organizational context and individualized service models. *Journal of Early Intervention, 22,* 185-199.

Pretti-Frontczak, K. & Bricker, D. (2001). Use of the embedding strategy during daily activities by early childhood education and early childhood special education teachers. *Infant-Toddler Intervention: The Transdisciplinary Journal, 11,* 111–128.

Raver, S. (2003). Keeping track: Using routines-based instruction and monitoring. *Young Exceptional Children, 6,* 12–20.

Raver, S. A. (2004). Monitoring child progress in early childhood special education settings. *Teaching Exceptional Children, 36*(6), 52-57.

Sandall, S., Hemmeter, M. L., Smith, B. J., & McLean, M. (Eds.). (2005). *DEC recommended practices: A comprehensive guide for practical application in early intervention/early childhood special education.* Missoula, MT: Division for Early Childhood.

Sandall, S. & Schwartz, I. (2008). *Building blocks for teaching preschoolers with special needs, second edition.* Baltimore: Brookes.

Shonkoff, J. & Phillips, D. (2000). *From neurons to neighborhoods: The science of early childhood development.* Washington, DC: National Academies Press.

Soukakou, E. (2012). Measuring quality in inclusive preschool classrooms: Development and validation of the Inclusive Classroom Profile (ICP). *Early Childhood Research Quarterly, 27,* 478-488.

Wolery, M., Brashers, M. S., & Nietzel, J. (2002). Ecological congruence assessment for classroom activities and routines: Identifying goals and intervention practices in childcare. *Topics in Early Childhood Special Education, 22,* 131-142.

Wolery, M. (2005). DEC Recommended practices: Child-focused practices. In S. Sandall, M.L. Hemmeter, B. J. Smith, & M. E. McLean (Eds.), *DEC recommended practices: A comprehensive guide for practical application* (pp. 71-106). Longmont, CO: Sopris.

Quality Instruction Through Complete Learning Trials

Blending Intentional Teaching With Embedded Instruction

Erin E. Barton, Ph.D.,
Vanderbilt University

Crystal Crowe Bishop, Ph.D.,

Patricia Snyder, Ph.D.,
University of Florida

Rochelle is a preschool teacher in an inclusive classroom at Bright Horizons Learning Center. She has fourteen 3- and 4-year-olds enrolled in her classroom. Rochelle prides herself on being an intentional teacher. Most of the children in her classroom are making progress toward acquiring knowledge and skills reflected in the state's preschool learning standards; however, she noticed children who seemed to be having difficulty playing cooperatively with one another. Rochelle has introduced some stories and discussion in large group about how to play with friends in the classroom, but Ally and Taegan still seem to be having challenges taking turns and sharing with friends. Likewise, Dylan plays mostly by himself and avoids playing with peers. In addition, Michael does not seem to be making much progress toward his IEP goals, which include interacting with peers, recognizing his letters, and building his expressive vocabulary. Michael usually ends up playing by himself during playtime, and Rochelle is having a hard time encouraging him to initiate play interactions with friends. Rochelle recently attended a workshop about embedded instruction and realized this is an approach she can blend with intentional teaching.

★ Current recommended practices endorse the full inclusion of children with disabilities with their typically developing peers with the appropriate supports to promote their learning and development (Division for Early Childhood [DEC], 2014; DEC/National Association for the Education of Young Children [NAEYC], 2009). Within inclusive classrooms, there often is a blending of teaching approaches to address the needs of all young children. Practitioners in inclusive classrooms must identify not only what to teach but how to teach to ensure that all children have access to and participate in the general preschool curriculum while meeting individualized learning needs. Grisham-Brown, Pretti-Frontczak, Hawkins, and Winchell (2009) define *blending* as an approach in which the curriculum is purposefully blended across ability levels and learning opportunities to set the stage for teaching all children in inclusive classrooms. For the purpose of this manuscript, we define *inclusion* using the DEC/NAEYC (2009) joint position statement on inclusion, which emphasizes that the defining features of quality, inclusive programs involve access, participation, and supports. This position statement specifies that inclusion involves children's access to a wide range of learning opportunities, activities, settings, and environments and incorporates the use of individualized accommodations, supports, and teaching to ensure their full participation in play and learning activities with peers and adults.

One teaching approach, intentional teaching, has been described as an integral component of developmentally appropriate practice ([DAP]; Copple & Bredekamp, 2009). Intentional teaching is an approach asserting that effective teachers recognize and respond to all opportunities to engage in and extend children's learning while also purposefully organizing the learning environment to create learning opportunities for children (Epstein, 2007, 2014). Thus, intentional teachers capitalize on children's motivation and engagement and use both child-initiated and teacher-initiated opportunities for learning (Epstein, 2007, 2014).

Another teaching approach, embedded instruction, is characterized as an approach to providing planned and systematic instruction during contextually relevant, ongoing activities and routines to support child engagement and learning (Snyder, Hemmeter, McLean, Sandall, & McLaughlin, 2013). Embedded instruction is a recommended practice in early intervention/early childhood special education ([EI/ECSE]; DEC, 2014; Wolery, 2005) in which teachers plan for and embed a *sufficient number* of instructional trials across the day for those children who need additional and often individualized instructional support. Instructional trials are referred to as complete learning trials (CLTs). This terminology emphasizes the importance of considering the teaching prompt or cue *and* the feedback or consequence provided to the child when providing instructional trials. Embedded instruction has been established to be effective for teaching a variety of skills in inclusive preschool classrooms. For example, embedded instruction has been used to teach social skills (Venn et al., 1993), academic skills (Daugherty, Grisham-Brown, & Hemmeter, 2001; Horn, Lieber, Li, Sandall, & Schwartz, 2000), and language skills (Grisham-Brown, Schuster, Hemmeter, & Collins, 2000) to young children in inclusive preschool classrooms.

★ Blending intentional teaching with embedded instruction leads to quality instruction for all young children in inclusive preschool classrooms. Blending these two approaches includes setting the occasion for children's learning (i.e., organizing the learning environment to provide learning opportunities) and ensuring sufficient opportunities to respond (i.e., CLT). The purposes of this article are to describe how to blend intentional teaching and embedded instruction approaches and to provide guidance for practitioners to plan for, implement, and evaluate CLTs during contextually relevant activities, routines, and transitions.

> *Blending intentional teaching with embedded instruction leads to quality instruction for all young children in inclusive preschool classrooms.*

Embedded Instruction

Four considerations are relevant for implementing embedded instruction (Snyder et al., 2013; Wolery, n.d.):

1. *What to teach* refers to the content of instruction. This involves the development of instructional learning targets that are (a) aligned with the general preschool curriculum; (b) functional, which means they are related to skills children will need to participate in naturally occurring daily activities and routines; (c) generative, which refers to skills that can be used across settings, materials, and people; (d) and measurable, which means the learning target is defined in such a way that the teacher can monitor the child's progress and make data-based decisions about instruction.

2. *When to teach* refers to the processes teachers use to identify relevant instructional contexts in which they can embed learning opportunities targeting a child's or group of children's individualized learning targets. Activity matrices often are used to specify when teaching will occur (see Figure 1).

3. *How to teach* refers to the processes teachers use to identify instructional procedures to align with the learning target skill, the child's phase of learning, and the child's learning history. Phases of learning include acquisition (learning how to do a skill), fluency (learning to do the skill smoothly and at natural rates), maintenance (doing the skill after instruction has ended), and generaliza-

tion (using the skill across different activities, people, materials, or contexts [Wolery, 2005]).

4. *How to evaluate* refers to the processes by which teachers collect data to determine (a) whether they are implementing embedded instruction practices as planned, (b) whether the child is making progress toward the learning target skill, and (c) whether changes to the implementation of embedded instruction practices are needed. Ongoing progress monitoring is a critical part of embedded instruction.

Figure 1
Example of a Classroom Activity Matrix

	Michael	Taegan	Ally	Dylan
Arrival	Name–1 trial			
Morning meeting	Name–1			
Centers	Request–8			Play 1 min–8
Lunch	Name–1			
	Request–4			
Small group	Request–3	Turns–4	Turns–4	
Snack	Name–1			
	Request–3			
Circle	Name–1	Turns–1	Turns–1	
Departure	Name–1			

Note. This activity matrix shows how many learning trials are planned to address each of the learning targets for the four children in Rochelle's classroom across all the activities in the daily schedule. Adapted from *Tools for Teachers: Planning Module*, by S. Sandall, P. Snyder, M. McLean, M. L. Hemmeter, T. McLaughlin, L. Edelman, and Embedded Instruction for Early Learning Project, 2009, Gainesville: University of Florida. Copyright 2009 by Embedded Instruction for Early Learning Project. Adapted with permission.

Complete Learning Trials

In embedded instruction, the term *complete learning trial* is used for a three-term contingency that includes a naturally occurring or planned antecedent (A) that sets the occasion for a child behavior (B) and is followed by a naturally occurring or planned feedback or consequence (C) (VanDerHeyden, Snyder, Smith, Sevin, & Longwell, 2005). In addition to the three-term contingency for the child, there are also three-term contingencies for the teacher. The series of interlocking adult and child

Figure 2
Illustration of Learn Unit and Complete Learning Trial as Interlocking Three-Term Contingencies

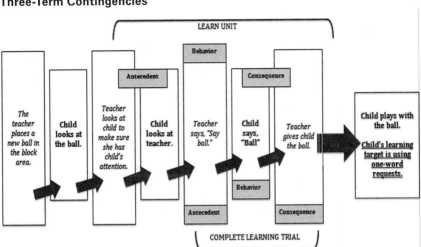

three-term contingencies has been described as a *learn unit* (Albers & Greer, 1991; Greer, 2002; Greer & McDonough, 1999; Vargus & Vargus, 1991). Figure 2 illustrates the relationship between a learn unit and a CLT.

A CLT is defined specifically as the child's three-term contingency. The learn unit includes the interlocking child and adult three-term contingencies. Learn units can be described in terms of teacher and child responses: The child's attention/engagement (e.g., in Figure 2 the child reaches for the ball) elicits a prompt from the teacher to the child (e.g., the teacher says, "Say ball") which elicits a response from the child (the child says "ball"), which in turn elicits feedback from the teacher (the teacher gives the child the ball). Greer and colleagues found a positive relation between teachers' rates of accurately implemented learn units and student outcomes (Greer & McDonough, 1999).

An intentional teacher using embedded instruction organizes the learning environment and uses systematic prompting and feedback (within these learn units) so CLTs will emerge for the child. For example referring back to the opening vignette, Rochelle might notice Michael playing near Dylan at the water table and say, "Michael, Dylan wants a turn with the blue bucket." If Michael looks at Dylan and gives him the bucket, she might say, "You gave Dylan a turn! That's being a good friend." Thus, Rochelle waited for Michael to attend, provided a prompt, and gave immediate feedback about his behavior. CLTs follow this structure, emphasize children's learning target behaviors, and are provided in contextually relevant situations (see Table 1).

Table 1
Examples of Complete Learning Trials (CLTs)

	Antecedent	Child Behavior	Consequence
Planned	When child is looking at the teacher, the teacher uses a gesture to prompt child to look at the child's visual schedule.	The child walks over to visual schedule and removes the next activity card, which is water play.	The teacher says, "Yes, Carly, it's time for water play!"
	The teacher hands the child a puzzle piece and says, "It's your turn!"	The child puts the puzzle piece in the puzzle.	The teacher smiles and says, "It fits! That is where it goes!"
	The teacher says to the small group of children, "What sounds do you hear in bus?" while pointing to the letters B-U-S and a picture of a bus.	The children respond "/b/!"	The teacher smiles and says, "Yep! Bus starts with the /b/ sound."
Naturally Occurring	The teacher rings the bell, which signals the transition to cleanup time.	Children start cleaning up toys.	Once toys are cleaned up, the children can wash hands for snack.
	The teacher pours all children a little bit of juice and puts the jug of juice on the counter next to the table.	A child drinks his juice, points to the juice, and asks for more.	The teacher immediately pours the child a little more juice.
	The teacher picks a child's name out of the name box to be song helper during circle time.	The child recognizes her name and comes to the front of circle and picks a song.	The teacher and children start singing the song she selected.
Mixed	(Planned) At the end of circle, the teacher says, "All children wearing red today can line up to go outside." She looks at Devonte and says, "You have bright red shoes on today!"	Devonte stands up.	(Naturally occurring) Devonte leaves circle time and lines up with peers near the door to go outside.

Table 1 (*continued*)

	Antecedent	Child Behavior	Consequence
Mixed	(Naturally occurring) The teacher sits next to the child in the block area and starts stacking blocks with the child.	The child continues stacking blocks and says, "It's tall!"	The teacher says, "Yes! Your building is SO tall, Molly!"
	(Naturally occurring) The teacher puts out just two scissors at the art table for all six children to use.	Jose turns to June and says, "Scissors please?"	The teacher physically helps June give Jose the scissors and says, "Wow! You all are sharing so well!"

Planning for CLTs: Considering Antecedents and Consequences

CLTs are effective when teachers intentionally plan the antecedent (e.g., teaching prompts) and consequence (e.g., feedback) in relation to an individual child's or group of children's learning targets, learning phase, and the instructional context. In blending intentional teaching and embedded instruction, teachers support child initiation and exploration *and* intentionally and systematically implement sufficient numbers of CLTs focused on identified learning targets. This does not mean teachers simply take advantage of "teachable moments." A teachable moment implies the onus is on the child to create a learning opportunity or suggests the teacher waits for these opportunities to occur. Although capitalizing on teachable moments is important and intentional teachers recognize and use child-initiated opportunities to expand a child's learning and development throughout the day, young children with disabilities might not engage with the environment in appropriate and meaningful ways to create a sufficient number of teachable moments to ensure learning (Carta, Schwartz, Atwater, & McConnell, 1991). Thus, effective teachers in inclusive classrooms use blended instruction to systematically and intentionally design the environment and plan what, when, and how to embed CLTs to ensure each child receives multiple, meaningful instructional opportunities. The onus is on the teacher to ensure each child is engaged, participating, learning new skills, and practicing mastered skills.

Environmental arrangements/modifications

For some learning targets and some children, the teacher can intentionally arrange the physical or social environment to set the occasion for CLTs.

Environmental arrangements set the occasion for child-guided learning through children's engagement and participation in everyday activities and routines (see Table 2). That is, intentional teachers arrange the environment to support child-guided learning when, for example, children are motivated to explore new materials, ask their peers for help or watch their peers model new behaviors, or focus on solving problems on their own (Epstein, 2007, 2014). Examples might include using materials related to a child's specific interests, arranging the physical environment so a child who uses a walker can stand next to peers at the same level at the water table, and adapting art materials for a child with low muscle tone to ensure he or she can grasp and use them independently with peers. The environment also can be arranged to occasion child initiations. For example, an environmental arrangement for Michael might include putting preferred toys in the water table to encourage his play near peers or adding extra paintbrushes to the easel when he is painting to encourage peers to paint near him.

Thus, effective teachers in inclusive classrooms use blended instruction to systematically and intentionally design the environment and plan what, when, and how to embed CLTs to ensure each child receives multiple, meaningful instructional opportunities.

Instructional Procedures

In inclusive classrooms, teachers who are blending intentional teaching and embedded instruction approaches will have to use more adult-guided instruction when children are unlikely to initiate, learn a skill, or have an experience on their own. Teachers might use three types of instructional procedures to initiate child learning. Teachers select different types of instructional procedures to use depending on the child's learning history and the specific learning target.

Antecedent-focused procedures. Antecedent-focused procedures or prompts (e.g., modeling a new skill, showing a child what to do, using a visual) focus on the "A" of the CLT and involve changing the prompts or enhancing the way the teacher delivers the prompts to ensure the child acquires and maintains a skill related to the learning target behavior. The goal should always be to decrease (i.e., fade) the use of the adult's added prompt to use what naturally prompts the learning target behavior. Thus, prompts need to be intentionally designed and systematically decreased over time.

Table 2
Type and Examples of Environmental Arrangements/Modifications

Type	Description	Example(s)
Environmental modifications		
Physical	Change the physical environment to promote independence.	Using a step stool at the sink so all children can reach the faucet.
Temporal	Change the schedule order, routines, or time for activities to accommodate all children.	Shortening circle time to ensure all children can participate in the entire routine.
Materials	Modify the instructional materials or media so all children can use.	Use larger-print books with tactile features for children with visual impairments.
Task/requirements	Alter the requirements of a task or activity to ensure the child's success.	Give the child paper with her name already outlined so she can trace or copy.
Special equipment	Provide specialized equipment to ensure the child's participation and independence.	Give the child with low muscle tone a chair with a back during circle time so he can observe and participate.
Environmental arrangements		
Choices	Plan for natural opportunities to provide the child with a meaningful choice during ongoing activities and routines. Adapt choices based on the child's skills and preferences.	Do you want the spoon or the fork to eat? Dolls or puzzles?
Preferred, novel/interesting materials	Use novel or preferred materials and rotate materials to promote interest and engagement.	1. Put new cups, bowls, and spoons in the sand table. 2. Rotate the blocks (use plastic, wooden, colored, and different sizes). 3. Dye the modeling clay purple (the child's favorite color).
In view/out of reach	Place preferred or necessary items in view but out of reach and wait for the children to ask for them or ask for help to get them.	1. Put the paintbrushes near the easel on a high shelf. 2. Place most of the toys for the modeling clay in a clear plastic container that is hard to open.
Inadequate portions	Give the children a small amount at a time and wait for them to ask for more.	1. Give a small amount of paint at the easel. 2. Give a smaller than usual amount of modeling clay.
Unexpected, silly situations	Create situations that are unexpected or violate the child's expectations and wait for them to protest.	1. Start to put the child's boots on your own feet. 2. Place the child's coat in the wrong cubby.

Note. Adapted from Kaiser, Ostrosky, and Alpert (1993); Sandall and Schwartz (2008).

For example, consider the system of least prompts, which starts with the natural prompt and gradually increases the adult prompting and instruction. The teacher initially would use the natural prompt and then use increasingly more guidance until the child demonstrates the learning target behavior. Using this procedure, prompts are decreased (i.e., faded) over time until a natural prompt sets the occasion for the behavior to occur. For example, when teaching Dylan play skills, Rochelle might place the toys on the floor in front of him (natural prompt), then give him a choice of toys (second prompt), then model a play behavior (third prompt), then use hand-over-hand assistance to help him play (Barton & Pavilanis, 2012). If he engages in play at any point during the instructional trial, Rochelle would stop her prompting and provide specific feedback (e.g., "You fed your hungry baby!") to complete the learning trial. In contrast, most-to-least prompting starts with the most directive prompt and gradually decreases the adult prompting and instruction. This means the teacher delivers the most intrusive prompt first, but decreases her guidance over time as the child learns the skill. With both the system of least prompts and most-to-least prompting, the specific types of prompts (e.g., verbal, physical, visual) are chosen based on the child's learning history and the context.

Time delay. Time delay is an additional antecedent-based procedure that can be embedded into typical routines and activities to teach new skills. With time delay, the teacher initially provides the natural prompt but immediately follows with the complete guidance (i.e., the controlling prompt or the most intrusive prompt needed to ensure the target behavior occurs). After delivering several of these CLTs, the teacher starts waiting either a constant or progressively longer amount of time between delivering the natural prompt and complete guidance.

Although the focus of all the aforementioned procedures is on changing the teacher's prompt, the instructional procedures are not effective unless the teacher also provides feedback immediately following the child's behavior. Without feedback, the CLTs are incomplete and might be ineffective regardless of the prompt. Consequence strategies involve systematic manipulation of the portion of the three-term contingency (i.e., the "C") that follows the behavior. This might include using specific positive reinforcement schedules (e.g., reinforcing every third behavior or reinforcing the child every minute for participating in circle), extra help (i.e., systematically delivering different feedback based on the child response), and shaping (i.e., differential reinforcement of successive approximations of the learning target). For example, shaping might be used to teach a Michael to request using one word. If Michael is playing with blocks, Rochelle might hold up a block and say "block." At first, Rochelle might give Michael the block (consequence) just for looking at her and the block. Over time, she might give him the block as a consequence for pointing to it, then only after he makes the /b/ or /ck/ sound, and finally when he attempts to say "block." The CLT in this example is Rochelle showing the block (i.e., antecedent), Michael looking at the block, making sounds, or saying "block," (i.e., behaviors successively reinforced), and Rochelle giving Michael the block (i.e., consequence). Shaping teaches Michael to say "block" in a meaningful context. Rochelle will intentionally embed multiple, direct CLTs like this during the day to ensure Michael masters the learning target behavior (i.e., uses one-word phrases).

Chaining. Chaining is another type of instructional strategy that might be effective for some children, particularly when the learning target involves sequences of behavior like drinking from a cup or washing hands. Chaining involves a specific sequence of behaviors identified through a task analysis (i.e., breaking a task down into small steps and reinforcing each step). For example, if a child is learning to drink from a cup, we might identify grasping the cup, bringing it to his or her mouth, and drinking as three discrete behaviors in a "drinks from a cup" chain. Each behavior (i.e., grasp the cup, bring to mouth, drink) occurs in sequence immediately after the previous and all are related to each other. A cup on a table (an environmentally arranged "A") might set the occasion for the child to grasp the cup (i.e., first discrete behavior). Grasp of the cup is both a reinforcer for grasping ("C") and the stimulus ("A") for bring to mouth (second discrete response). This sequence continues until the child drinks from the cup. Washing hands, getting dressed, and brushing teeth are additional examples of learning targets that might be taught using chaining.

Naturalistic instructional procedures. Naturalistic instructional procedures including incidental teaching, naturalistic time delay, and milieu teaching can be embedded into a variety of routines and activities to teach a range of skills (Kaiser & Hester, 1994; McGee, Morrier, & Daly, 1999). Incidental teaching can be used to improve young children's communication skills. The teacher sets up the environment to elicit a request from the child, waits for the child to initiate, and then prompts the target response. For example, Rochelle might plan to give Michael choices during snack, circle time, and transitions to build his expressive vocabulary. During snack she gives him just a few crackers, waits for him to point to the crackers, and provides him the choice between, for example, crackers or a juice. If he says "cracker" or "juice" she gives him the item. If he points at one of them, she says the word for the item he pointed at ("Cracker, please") and waits. If he says "cracker" she gives it to him and says, "You want more crackers!" If he points again, she says "Cracker, please!" and gives him the cracker. In this manner, Rochelle provides a contextually relevant learning opportunity based on a functional learning target with naturally occurring consequence.

Similarly, with naturalistic time delay, the teacher waits a specified amount of time before providing the prompt. For example, Rochelle might plan to use time delay to help Michael learn the letters in his name. She might use placemats with each child's name during snack. When Michael comes to the table looking for his placement she might point to the letter "M" and say, "Michael starts with a ___ " and waits a specified amount of time for him to respond. If he says, "M" she gives him the placemat and says, "Yes! Michael starts with a M!" If he does not say anything or says the wrong letter, she says, "M, Michael starts with a M" and gives him the placemat. The naturalistic instructional procedures require waiting for the child to initiate. Teachers might need to use the other antecedent- or consequence-based strategies previously described with children who initiate at low rates or are unlikely to initiate.

Planning, Implementing, and Evaluating Embedded Instruction

Teachers using a blended instructional approach need to intentionally plan for, implement, and evaluate embedded instruction. Intentional teachers arrange the environment to support child-guided learning, provide adult-guided instruction using CLTs, and systematically monitor progress over time. In the sections below, we describe strategies related to planning, implementing, and evaluating embedded instruction.

Creation of the Written Implementation Plan

As part of being an intentional teacher using a blended approach, it is important to create a written plan detailing the implementation of CLTs for each child or group of children. This might include a list of the daily routines and activities and specific plans for which instructional procedures to use and how many CLTs to embed on which learning target behavior within each activity across the day. The written forms should allow the teacher to plan and monitor implementation. Once the plans are created, it is important to review the opportunities for CLTs and ensure they are sufficient to promote child learning. Figure 1 is an example of an activity matrix showing how many trials Rochelle has planned to implement for Michael, Taegan, Ally, and Dylan. Activity matrices can be created to show how many CLTs are planned for multiple children across the entire daily schedule, as shown in Figure 1, or they can be created for specific activities (e.g., centers, circle), areas of the classroom (e.g., sensory table, block area, dramatic play area), or for an individual child. Activity matrices should be used in conjunction with instructional plans, which provide more detailed information about the what, the how, and the when for an entire learning cycle for the child (e.g., acquisition, fluency, maintenance, and generalization). Figure 3 is an example of a planning form that allows a teacher to focus on one learning target for a child, consider when and how to embed across the day, and includes a section for progress monitoring.

Figure 3
Example of an Instructional Planning Sheet. Adapted From *Tools for Teachers: Planning Module*, by S. Sandall, P. Snyder, M. McLean, M. L. Hemmeter, T. McLaughlin, L. Edelman, and Embedded Instruction for Early Learning Project, 2009, Gainesville: University of Florida. Copyright 2009 by Embedded Instruction for Early Learning Project. Adapted With Permission.

Instructional Planning Sheet

Child's Name: Michael

Learning Target: Use at least two words to request objects or food

Routines/Activities: Centers, Lunch, Snack, Small Groups

Materials: Preferred toys, food items at snack, critical materials to complete activities in small groups

Antecedent	Behavior	Consequence
What do you say or do?	What does the child do?	How do you respond?
Place toy/material/food in view but out of reach	Use at least 2 words two request the item (e.g., want ball, need paper, eat cookie)	Provide verbal feedback (you can have the cookie, thank you for asking me)
Ask What do you want?		Give item
What, if any, assistance, do you provide?		If incorrect: Say _____ _____ Model 2-word request

Data collection:

Activity	CLT Planned	CLT Delivered	Correct Response
Centers	8	1 1 1 1	1 1
Lunch	4	1 1	1
Small Group	3	1	1
Snack	3	1 1	1

Rochelle writes a plan to embed CLTs for Ally, Taegan, Dylan, and Michael. With Ally and Taegan, she works on taking turns with peers by embedding CLTs into small- and large-group activities. At centers, she will space CLTs with Dylan to help him engage in play with a toy for at least 1 minute. To help Michael with his expressive vocabulary, Rochelle will distribute CLTs to elicit two-word requests for objects or food at snack time, small group, and centers. She also will work on letter recognition by distributing CLTs for Michael to recognize his printed name at arrival, circle, snack, and departure. Now she can work on implementing her plan.

Implementation of CLTs

The key to blending intentional teaching and embedded instruction is that a sufficient number of CLTs are delivered, as intended, into ongoing activities for those children who need extra learning supports. CLTs can be implemented for an individual child or groups of children during planned and naturally occurring activities. This ensures that children receive the appropriate amount of teaching focused on their learning targets. Implementation can begin once the learning targets for groups and individual children are identified and instruction is planned. The planning should guide the when, how, and number of CLTs to embed. Table 3 provides a summary of the steps for using CLTs.

Delivery of CLTs. CLTs can be massed, spaced, or distributed within meaningful contexts (see Tables 4 and 5 for examples; Wolery, Ault, & Doyle, 1992). Massed CLTs are delivered as consecutive, discrete CLTs within an activity or routine. Spaced CLTs are also delivered within an

Table 3
Steps for Using Complete Learning Trials (CLTs)

1.	Assess each child's present level of development and learning history.
2.	Plan to provide a sufficient number of embedded CLTs for each child.
3.	Plan how to deliver CLTs; they can be massed, spaced, or distributed within meaningful contexts based on the needs of the child, the learning target, and the context, including what skills are needed for access and participation in typical activities and routines.
4.	Consider how the learning target behavior is related to one of these three ultimate outcomes: (1) acquiring and using knowledge and skills, (2) having positive social-emotional skills, and (3) using appropriate behaviors to meet their needs.

activity or routine; however, there is a noninstructional pause between CLTs. Distributed CLTs are embedded within or across routines and activities. Massed, spaced, or distributed CLTs are delivered based on the context (i.e., the expectations within the activity), the child's learning targets, and the phase of learning. Children might need massed CLTs if they are just learning a skill related to a learning target behavior and distributed CLTs if they are generalizing a skill.

For example, massed instruction includes the presentation of quick, consecutive, discrete CLTs within an activity or routine. These might be appropriate for teaching Michael to request items during snack, where there are multiple opportunities for him to request. Rochelle might place a small amount of snack on his plate and wait for him to ask for more, give him more, and repeat multiple times. Spaced CLTs are often appropriate during small-group activities or routines and include delivering CLTs to a child or children with a brief pause without instruction between CLTs. For example, Rochelle might pass Ally the "turn card," comment on her turn (e.g., "You picked two apple cards!"), and help her pass the turn card to Taegan. Because Ally and Taegan are still learning to take turns, Rochelle might provide a verbal or gestural prompt and specific feedback. Using this strategy, each child has multiple, meaningful opportunities to learn how to take turns or practice taking turns spaced throughout the engaging, developmentally appropriate game. Distributed CLTs are delivered within and across activities. For example, Rochelle might embed multiple CLTs for Michael to identify his name across routines. During arrival, she might put a label with his name on his cubby and say, "Which cubby is yours, Michael?" When Michael identifies his name, she says, "Yes! That says 'Michael'" and spells out M-i-c-h-a-e-l. During snack, she might use placements with each child's name. She might say, "Whose is this?" and hold up Michael's placemat. She can deliver the same type of consequence used during arrival here. During the transition to circle time, she might use carpet squares with name labels. She might say, "Whose is this?" and hold up Michael's carpet square. Again, she can deliver the same consequence. Thus, distributed CLTs for the same learning target can be embedded across activities, routines, and transitions using a sufficient number of CLTs, which promotes both acquisition and generalization.

Intentional teachers arrange the environment to support child-guided learning, provide adult-guided instruction using CLTs, and systematically monitor progress over time.

Table 4
Examples of Embedding Complete Learning Trials (CLTs) for Group Activities

Learning target	Massed CLTs	Spaced CLTs	Distributed CLTs
Children will give peers a turn during a game	The teacher repeats this with Mikayla several times in a row counting to three to five each time. Mikayla receives at least 8–10 massed complete learning trials in a row.	Set up a simple board game with three or four children. Each child takes a turn rolling a large die and moving her or his game piece. A: Teacher says, "It's Mark's turn. Give the die to Mark." B: Josie passes the die to Mark and Mark rolls the die. C: "Nice sharing Josie! What number is Mark going to roll?" The teacher repeats this with each child and adapts the prompts and feedback based on the individual child's needs. The children recieve at least 9–10 spaced complete learning trials during the activity.	The teacher will set up opportunities for peers to take turns throughout several activities during the day. She will put just two shovels in the sand table, allow just one child at the computer at a time for 5 minutes, allow just 2 children at the easel at a time, and put just two rollers at the modeling clay table. A: Teacher says, "Mark can have the shovel for 2 more minutes then its Toma's turn." She sets a visual timer. After two minutes she says, "It's Toma's turn." B: Mark passes the shovel to Toma. C: "Nice sharing Mark! What number is Toma going to make?" The teacher repeats this with each child and adapts the prompts and feedback based on the individual child's needs. Each child receives at least 10 distributed complete learning trials during the day.

Table 4 (continued)

Learning target	Massed CLTs	Spaced CLTs	Distributed CLTs
Children will comment on pictures and events in the book.	Read a story with props and a felt board to just Luke. He places a prop on the felt board that corresponds with the events in the story.	Read a story with props and a felt board to 3–4 students. Each child takes a turn placing a prop on the felt board that corresponds with the events in the story.	The teacher will read books to the children at least three different times during the day (e.g., small group time, circle time, and the transition to departure). She will make sure each child has an opportunity to comment at least twice during each book each day.
	A: Teacher says, "Brown bear, brown bear what do you see? Luke, what does the brown bear see?" and points to the red bird.	A: Teacher says, "Brown bear, brown bear what do you see? Who has the brown bear?" and points to Luke.	A: Teacher says, "The driver on the bus goes . . . Maci, what does the driver do next?
	B: Luke holds up the red bird, places it on the felt board, and says, "red bird!"	B: Luke holds up the brown bear, places it on the felt board, and says, "brown bear!"	B: Maci points to the book and says, "Beep, beep, beep"
	C: "Yes, brown bear saw the red bird!"	C: "Yes, Luke had the brown bear!"	C: "Yes! The driver on the bus goes Beep beep beep!"
	The teacher repeats this with Luke for each page. Luke receives at least 8–10 massed complete learning trials in a row.	The teacher repeats this for each page and each child and adapts the prompts and feedback based on the individual child's needs. The children receive at least 5–6 spaced complete learning trials during the book. If more complete learning trials are needed, the teacher can read the book twice and give children different props the second time.	The teacher repeats this with each child and adapts the prompts and feedback based on the individual child's needs. Each child receives at least 5–6 distributed complete learning trials during the day.

Table 5
Examples of Embedding Complete Learning Trials (CLTs) for Individual Activities

Learning target	Spaced CLTs	Massed CLTs	Distributed CLTs
Mikayla will count to 5 using toys or other items by pointing to each item and saying the number.	The teacher will sit next to Mikayla and peers in the block area. She will play with the blocks and follow Mikayla's lead in play.	The teacher will sit next to Mikayla during snack time. She serves small Goldfish for snack and only gives Mikayla four to five at time.	The teacher plans to embed CLTs for counting into at least four activities for Mikayla. The teacher will prompt counting during snack, block play, water play, and outside on the playground.
	A: Teacher says, "That is a long train track! Let's count the blocks, points to the first one says, and says, "One . . ." She waits for Mikayla to imitate and keep counting.	A: After Mikayla eats one or two Goldfish, the teacher says, "Let's count how many are left. One . . ."	A: While Mikayla is in the sandbox outside with acorns and sand, the teacher says, "That is a lot of acorns Mikayla! How many do you have? One . . ."
	B: Mikayla says, "One, two . . ."	B: Mikayla says, "One, two, three . . ."	B: Mikayla says, "One, two, three . . ."
	C: "There are five blocks lined up!"	C: "There are three left! Want two more?" and counts one, two.	C: "You have four acorns!"
	The teacher repeats this with Mikayla after pausing and interacting with a different child. Mikayla receives at least five spaced CLTs during block play.	The teacher repeats this with Mikayla several times in a row, counting to three to five each time. Mikayla receives at least 8–10 massed CLTs in a row.	The teacher repeats this with Mikayla again on the playground and during other activities. Mikayla receives more than 10 distributed CLTs throughout the day.

Table 5 (*continued*)

Learning target	Spaced CLTs	Massed CLTs	Distributed CLTs
Louis will take 10 independent steps.	The teacher will set up a ball game with Louis and two peers on the playground. The teacher will throw the ball and the child will try to toss it in the hoop. then go get it and pass to the next child. After Louis takes a turn, she prompts him to walk about five steps to get the ball and five steps back to bring to a peer. A: Teacher says, "Louis's ball made it in the hoop! Its Sammy's turn!" B: Louis walks five steps to the hoop and five steps back! C: The teacher says, "Its Sammy's turn! Nice shot Louis!" The teacher repeats this with each child. Louis receives at least 10 spaced CLTs during the ball game.		The teacher plans to embed CLTs for walking into at least five activities or transitions for Louis. The teacher will prompt walking during the transition at arrival, and snack time, outdoor play, and circle time. A: During circle time, the teacher picks Louis's name out of the bag to pick a song. She says, "Louis come up here and pick a song!" B: Louis walks about five steps to the front of circle, picks a song, and walks about five steps back to his spot when finished. C: "You picked the popcorn song!" The teacher repeats this with Louis again on the playground and during other activities. Louis receives more than 10 distributed CLTs throughout the day.

Individual and group activities. Typical early childhood class-rooms include a mix of individual and group activities. Embedded instruction can be implemented in both types of instructional settings (see Tables 4 and 5). For example, CLTs focused on the overall goal of the activity and each child's individual learning targets can be embedded into group activities. With careful planning and systematic instruction, group activities can provide multiple opportunities for spaced or massed CLTs depending on the context. Furthermore, group activities provide opportunities for observational learning (Ledford, Gast, Luscre, & Ayers, 2008). Some children will exhibit a behavior after watching and imitating other children. However, other children might need individualized instruction. In either situation, it is essential to secure the child's attention prior to implementing the CLT. This is particularly important during group activities.

Planned versus naturally occurring CLTS. In high-quality, well-planned classrooms with intentional teachers, there will be opportunities for both naturally occurring and planned CLTs. However, as described previously, even naturally occurring CLTs require intentional planning. When children are first acquiring skills, they might need more planned CLTs embedded into ongoing activities. However, as children become fluent in target skills, teachers can fade prompt-based antecedents and thin the consequences to ensure naturally occurring antecedent and consequences occasion and maintain the behavior.

Planned CLTs might be particularly important for young children with special needs. For example, at the beginning of the year, Rochelle's students might be learning to follow the transition cues. During the transition from snack to circle time, Rochelle says, "It's time to clean up. The red table can line up first." This is the naturally occurring antecedent. Most children at the red table know this means to pick up their plate and cup, place them in the sink, and line up to wash hands. Some children observe other children doing this and imitate them. The naturally occurring consequence might be that Rochelle smiles at them or says, "Pick your seat at circle!" after they finish washing hands. Michael and Dylan might need more support to learn this routine. For example, Rochelle might look at Dylan and point to the sink after saying, "It's the red table's turn to clean up." After he has cleaned up his plate and washed his hands, Rochelle also might say, "Dylan, you are all clean! Go pick a seat on the circle rug!" In this example, the naturally occurring CLTs are effective for some children, and Rochelle can embed individual CLTs into the transition to ensure all children are learning to independently follow the routine.

Evaluation of CLTs

An important component of effective blended instruction is evaluating the implementation of CLTs. Evaluating CLTs involves collecting data to determine whether teachers are implementing CLTs as intended and if a child or group of children is learning skills related to their learning targets. Although practitioners often think about collecting data to monitor child progress, it is equally important to examine whether the CLTs are implemented as planned. For example, Rochelle might collect data on the number of times Michael initiates an interaction with a peer and find that he has not made much improvement over the course of 2 weeks. One reason might be that the teaching procedures are not aligned with his current skill level. It might be that the teaching is appropriate, but the number of CLTs is not sufficient. Or, it could be that both the teaching procedures and the number of CLTs planned are appropriate, but the CLTs are not being implemented appropriately in terms of the prompts used or the consequences provided. Without collecting data on both Michael's progress and the implementation of the CLTs, it will be difficult for Rochelle to make informed decisions.

Collecting data on implementation. There are a number of ways teachers can collect and use data on their implementation of CLTs. Teachers can count the number of CLTs delivered for a learning target and compare it with the instructional plan. This might be useful in conjunction with child data to determine whether the number of CLTs is sufficient. This information also helps the teacher evaluate whether the instructional plan is being implemented as planned. It does not, however, give any information about whether the CLTs delivered were actually CLTs. For example, Rochelle might videotape herself implementing CLTs and then review the video to determine whether the CLTs were complete and which instructional procedures were used (Bishop, Snyder, & Crow, 2014; Crowe, Snyder, Crow, & Mullin, 2011). This method for collecting data provides information on both the implementation of CLTs and child behaviors and will help Rochelle make decisions about whether she needs to be more intentional in planning or implementing the components of a CLT or whether she might want to try a different instructional procedure.

Collecting child data. In addition to collecting data on implementation of CLTs, it is important to collect data to monitor children's progress toward their learning targets. There are several types of data that can be collected to monitor child progress, including the frequency with which the child demonstrates the target behavior within and across activities, the amount of time it takes a child to complete a task, the percentage of opportunities in which the child demonstrates the target behavior, what level of support is needed, or how fluent the child is in demonstrating the behavior. The type of data to collect and when to collect depends on the child's learning target, the instructional plan, and whether the goal is to assess acquisition, fluency, generalization, or maintenance. For example, if Rochelle determined that Ally is able to take turns with her peers when prompted during circle time, she might assess whether this skill is generalizing across activities and peers. Because Dylan's learning target involves engaging in play for at least 1 minute, Rochelle might want to time how long he engages in play routines with different toys. Child data should be used in conjunction with implementation data to determine whether changes are needed to the number of CLTs implemented, whether additional support is needed or prompting can be faded, and whether the child might be ready for a new target skill (Hojnoski, Gischlar, & Missall, 2009a, 2009b).

Rochelle decides to ask one of her assistants to videotape small-group time so she can monitor her implementation of CLTs for Ally, Taegan, and Michael. When she watches her video, she realizes she did implement CLTs for Ally and Taegan as planned, but she only delivered one learning trial for Michael's learning target when she had planned to deliver three. Although it was a CLT, she is not sure this is sufficient to help him acquire his target skill. She notices that Ally takes her own turn and allows her friend to have a turn after every verbal prompt. Taegan still needs additional prompts to give a peer a turn 50% of the time. Rochelle decides to continue giving verbal prompts to Taegan during small group but wants to start fading verbal prompts for Ally. In her revised instructional plan, Rochelle decides to try using a gestural prompt for Ally to take her turn. She realizes she needs to be more intentional about providing opportunities for Michael to request, so she decides to play a game with highly preferred materials that he can request. She also keeps her implementation plan on hand to tally the number of CLTs she implements during the activity. Rochelle continues to monitor her implementation of CLTs and child progress so she can make informed decisions about how to continue individualizing instruction.

Important Considerations for Using CLTs

There are several important factors teachers should consider when planning to deliver CLTs. First, teachers should make sure they understand each child's present level of development and learning history. This will help with identifying functional, developmentally appropriate learning targets and effective instructional procedures. For example, children with language delays might respond to visual or gestural prompts more efficiently than verbal prompts. Children with social delays might not respond to social praise at all; tangible items might be more effective. Second, teachers should ensure they are providing a sufficient number of CLTs for each child. This involves careful planning of all aspects of the environment and ongoing progress monitoring. Children need a mix of opportunities to learn new target behaviors and practice target behaviors already learned. If children are spending too much time not engaged or engaged with the same materials, it might indicate that the child needs more challenging activities or more learning opportunities. CLTs should be continually adapted to ensure children are maintaining skills and generalizing them across settings, activities, routines, materials, and people. Third, part of planning should involve determining how to deliver the CLTs. They can be massed, spaced, or distributed within meaningful contexts based on the needs of the child, the learning target, and the context. Finally, teachers should remember the ultimate outcomes from blended instruction focus on preschool children (1) acquiring and using knowledge and skills, including communication and early literacy; (2) having positive social-emotional skills, including social relationships; and (3) using appropriate behavior to meet their needs (Early Childhood Outcomes Center, 2005). As learning targets are identified, teachers should consider how the learning target behavior is related to one of these three functional and ultimate outcomes.

Note

For more information, please contact Erin E. Barton at erin.e.barton@vanderbilt.edu.

References

Albers, A. E. & Greer, D. (1991). Is the three-term contingency trial a predictor of effective instruction? *Journal of Behavioral Education, 1*, 337-354.

Barton, E. E. & Pavlanis, R. L. (2012). Teaching pretend play to young children with autism. *Young Exceptional Children, 15,* 5-17.

Bishop, C., Snyder, P. A., & Crow, R. (2014). *Impact of video self-monitoring on preschool teachers' implementation of complete learning trials.* Manuscript in preparation.

Carta, J. J., Schwartz, I. S., Atwater, J. B., & McConnell, S. R. (1991). Developmentally appropriate practice: Appraising its usefulness for young children with disabilities. *Topics in Early Childhood Special Education, 11,* 1-20.

Copple, C. & Bredekamp, S. (2009). *Developmentally appropriate practice in early childhood programs serving children from birth through age 8* (3rd ed.). Washington, DC: National Association for the Education of Young Children.

Crowe, C., Snyder, P., Mullin, M., Crow, R., & Embedded Instruction for Early Learning Project (2009). *Embedded instruction for early learning observation system–Teacher Version (EIOS-T).* [Manual and training videos]. Unpublished instrument, University of Florida, College of Education, Gainesville.

Daugherty, S., Grisham-Brown, J., & Hemmeter, M. L. (2001). The effects of embedded skill instruction on the acquisition of target and nontarget skills in preschoolers with developmental delay. *Topics in Early Childhood Special Education, 21,* 211-219.

DEC/NAEYC. (2009). *Early childhood inclusion: A joint position statement of the Division for Early Childhood (DEC) and the National Association for the Education of Young Children (NAEYC).* Chapel Hill: The University of North Carolina, FPG Child Development Institute.

Division for Early Childhood. (2014). *DEC recommended practices in early intervention/early childhood special education.* Retrieved May 14, 2014 from http://www.dec-sped.org/recommendedpractices

Early Childhood Outcomes Center. (2005, April). *Family and child outcomes for early intervention and early childhood special education*. Retrieved on January 15, 2014, from http://www.the-eco-center.org

Epstein, A. S. (2007). *The intentional teacher: Choosing the best strategies for young children's learning*. Washington, DC: National Association for the Education of Young Children.

Epstein, A. S. (2014). *The intentional teacher: Choosing the best strategies for young children's learning* (2nd ed.). Washington: National Association for the Education of Young Children.

Gischlar, K. L., Hojnoski, R. L., & Missall, K. N. (2009). Improving child outcomes with data based decision making: Interpreting and using data. *Young Exceptional Children, 13*, 2-18.

Greer, R. D. (2002). *Designing teaching strategies: An applied behavior analysis systems approach*. San Diego: Academic Press.

Greer, R. D. & McDonough, S. H. (1999). Is the learn unit a fundamental measure of pedagogy? *Behavior Analyst, 22,* 5–16.

Grisham-Brown, J., Schuster, J. W., Hemmeter, M. L., & Collins, B. C. (2000). Using an embedding strategy to teach preschoolers with significant disabilities. *Journal of Behavioral Education, 10,* 139-162.

Grisham-Brown, J. L., Pretti-Frontczak, K., Hawkins, S., & Winchell, B. (2009). An examination of how to address early learning standards for all children within blended preschool classrooms. *Topics in Early Childhood Special Education, 29,* 131-142.

Hojnoski, R. L., Gischlar, K. L., & Missall, K. N. (2009a). Improving child outcomes with data based decision making: Collecting data. *Young Exceptional Children, 12,* 32-44.

Hojnoski, R. L., Gischlar, K. L., & Missall, K. N. (2009b). Improving child outcomes with data-based decision making: Graphing data. *Young Exceptional Children, 12,* 15-30.

Horn, E., Lieber, J., Sandall, S., & Schwartz, I. (2001). Embedded learning opportunities as an instructional strategy for supporting children's learning in inclusive programs. *Young Exceptional Children Monograph Series, 3,* 59-70.

Kaiser, A. P. & Hester, P. P. (1994). Generalized effects of enhanced milieu teaching. *Journal of Speech and Hearing Research, 37,* 1320–1340.

Kaiser, A. P., Ostrosky, M. M., & Alpert, C. L. (1993). Training teachers to use environmental arrangement and milieu teaching with nonverbal preschool children. *Journal of the Association for Persons with Severe Handicaps, 18,* 188-199.

Ledford, J. R., Gast, D. L., Luscre, D., & Ayers, K. M. (2008). Observational and incidental learning by children with autism during small group instruction. *Journal of Autism and Developmental Disorders, 38,* 86-103.

McGee, G. G., Morrier, M. J., & Daly, T. (1999). An incidental teaching approach to early intervention for toddlers with autism. *Journal of the Association for Persons With Severe Handicaps, 24,* 133-146.

Sandall, S., Snyder, P., McLean, M., Hemmeter, M. L., McLaughlin, T., Edelman, L., & Embedded Instruction for Early Learning Project. (2009). *Tools for teachers: Planning module* [Trainer's Guide]. Unpublished professional development series. College of Education, University of Florida, Gainesville, FL.

Sandall, S. R. & Schwartz, I. S. (2008). *Building blocks for teaching preschoolers with special needs* (2nd ed.). Baltimore: Brookes.

Snyder, P., Hemmeter, M. L., McLean, M. E., Sandall, S., & McLaughlin, T. M. (2013). Embedded instruction to support early learning in response to intervention frameworks. In V. Buysse & E. S. Peisner-Feinberg (Eds.), *Handbook of response to intervention in early childhood* (pp. 283-300). Baltimore, MD: Brookes.

VanDerHeyden, A. M., Snyder, P., Smith, A., Sevin, B., & Longwell, J. (2005). Effects of complete learning trials on child engagement. *Topics in Early Childhood Special Education, 25,* 81-94.

Vargus, E. A. & Vargus, J. S. (1991). Programmed instruction: What it is and how to do it. *Journal of Behavioral Education, 1,* 235-251.

Venn, M. L., Wolery, M., Werts, M. G., Morris, A., DeCesare, L. D., & Cuffs, M. S. (1993). Embedding instruction in art activities to teach preschoolers with disabilities to imitate their peers. *Early Childhood Research Quarterly, 8,* 277-294.

Wolery, M. (2005). DEC recommended practices: Child-focused practices. In S. Sandall, M. L. Hemmeter, B. J. Smith, & M. E. McLean (Eds.), *DEC recommended practices: A comprehensive guide for practical application in early intervention/early childhood special education* (pp. 71-106). Missoula, MT: Division for Early Childhood.

Wolery, M. (n.d.). Embedding prompting strategies in inclusive preschool classes. Retrieved January 15, 2014, from http://ectacenter.org/topics/inclusion/research/rs_embed.asp#footnote

Wolery, M., Ault, M. J., & Doyle, P. M. (1992). *Teaching students with moderate to severe disabilities*. New York: Longman.

Delivering Individualized Instruction During Ongoing Classroom Activities and Routines

Three Success Stories

Jennifer Grisham-Brown, Ed.D.,
University of Kentucky

Kristie Pretti-Frontczak, Ph.D.,
B2K Solutions, Ltd.

Alicia Bachman, B.A., Corey Gannon, B.A., and Dorothy Mitchell, B.A.,
University of Kentucky

As her first year of teaching came to a close, Ms. Mattie felt good about the time spent building relationships with her highly diverse group of children and their families, managing the classroom environment, and planning meaningful activities to fill the day. However, as she "came up for air" and started to reflect on what she would do differently the next year, she knew that she was not implementing many of the practices she had learned in college. Sure, she completed an assessment on each child as dictated by her school district, but she had to admit that she really hadn't used the data to help her plan what to teach.

While she knew the children enjoyed the activities she planned, she felt like she was teaching the same concepts from the district curriculum (e.g., colors, shapes, numbers) to all of the children without individualizing or differentiating. It worried her that some children were probably not ready to learn the concepts she was teaching. Likewise, she worried that some children were not being challenged enough.

But HOW in the world was she supposed to support everyone in her classroom in the way in which they needed to be taught? She had 20 children in her class and one teaching assistant to help her! The children ranged *in age from 3 to 5 years. Of the 20 children, six children had disabilities, including two with Autism Spectrum Disorder. Although the remaining 14 children were "typically developing," three demonstrated challenging behavior and eight were English language learners. Ms. Mattie knew the importance of differentiating instruction, yet she struggled to find ways to address the more intensive needs of children in her classroom.*

Whether a first-year teacher, or a 20-year veteran, Ms. Mattie's situation is common in center-based early childhood programs[1] in the United States. As a country, the United States' population has become increasingly diverse, and subsequently, early childhood programs have become equally diverse. At least two other factors have diversified the makeup of children served in center-based programs. First, the mandate to serve infants and toddlers with disabilities in their natural environments has led to increased services delivered in community-based childcare programs. Second, increases in funding for pre-kindergarten (pre-K) programs, particularly for children who are at risk, has lead local education agencies to partner with community-based child care programs and Head Start programs in order to serve more children. With the increase in the diversity of children being served has come the increased need to diversify how programs operate, how they remain fiscally viable, and how best to deliver instruction.

One broad strategy has been to blend or combine resources, philosophies, and strategies. Programs following a blended approach commonly pull from a variety of sources in an effort to create a program that is as eclectic and versatile as the children and families served. For example, in a classroom following a blended approach a teacher may use real life materials in the kitchen area such as cereal boxes, menus from restaurants, and real cups and plates (pulling from the traditions of Maria Montessori). As well, she may also guide children through projects of interest to promote problem solving, creativity, and small group explorations (pulling from the traditions of Reggio Emilia). Lastly, she may promote learning and changes in behavior by systematically arranging the environment and providing individualized reinforcement to give children feedback (pulling from the traditions of classical and operant conditioning).

Programs following a blended approach commonly pull from a variety of sources in an effort to create a program that is as eclectic and versatile as the children and families served.

---

[1] We define center-based early childhood programs as those that serve children between the ages of birth to 8 years of age and may include childcare programs, publicly funded preschool, and kindergarten.

The purpose of this article is twofold. First, we aim to describe two key practices associated with a blended approach designed to meet the learning needs of children diverse abilities served in center-based programs. Second, we provide three illustrations of how children, particularly those with intensive learning needs, can successfully acquire important outcomes when served in classrooms using a blended approach.

Blended Programs and Classrooms

Grisham-Brown and colleagues (2005, 2013, 2014) define *blended programs* or *blended classrooms* as those having at least four defining characteristics. First, they serve a variety of children including those with identified disabilities, those from culturally and linguistically diverse backgrounds, and those from a wide range of socioeconomically situations. Second, they combine fiscal (e.g., Head Start funds; state pre-K dollars; IDEA Parts C and B 619 funds; and child care subsidies) and human resources to address the needs of children being served. Third, teachers in blended classrooms are ideally trained in the traditions of both early childhood education and early childhood special education. Finally, they combine philosophies and practices across four linked curricular elements including *assessment, scope and sequence, activities and instruction,* and *progress monitoring.* It is these four linked curricular elements, along with a supportive leadership team, collaborative partnerships, quality professional development, and an adherence to data-driven decision making, that comprise a blended approach, or what has been termed a "Curriculum Framework."

Teachers in blended classrooms may feel unable to abide by the preciseness of the procedures described in the literature due to the competing demands of their classrooms, including overcrowding, adherence to multiple state and federal mandates, and the diverse learning needs of children.

A curriculum framework is one illustration of how blended programs can design and deliver learning opportunities for diverse groups and individual children. To learn more about the characteristics of blended programs, particularly the blending of curricular elements as part of a curriculum framework, see Grisham-Brown et al. (2005), Grisham-Brown and Pretti-Frontczak (2011), and Grisham-Brown and Pretti-Frontczak (2013). While it is beyond the scope of this article to go into detail regarding the four characteristics of blended programs or to further illustrate blending through descriptions of a curriculum framework, we do describe two key aspects of blended programs: (1) *identifying outcomes* for each child in the classroom and (2) *selecting and delivering appropriate instructional strategies* to teach identified outcomes.

Identifying Outcomes

One of the issues teachers face when working in a blended classroom is determining "who needs to learn what." Because of the linguistic, cultural, and individual diversity found in a blended classroom, teachers are challenged to determine outcomes for a group of children whose development may go from 6 months to 6 years. In addition, individual children may have varying needs. For example, a child may have strengths in some developmental areas (e.g., getting wants and needs met, playing with other children) but may struggle in other developmental areas (e.g., using numbers, being understood by others). Further, the blending of funds cause teachers to become accountable to a variety of "masters" who set forth what children should learn. For example, receiving state dollars for pre-K requires accountability toward state early learning standards, serving children with disabilities under IDEA requires accountability toward outcomes on individualized plans, and receiving Head Start funds requires to accountability toward their Early Learning Framework standards. The wide range of learning needs presented by the children and the wide range of learning outcomes presented by funding agencies causes teachers to make multiple and varied instructional decisions about what to teach diverse groups of children as well as each individual child.

One of the issues teachers face when working in a blended classroom is determining "who needs to learn what".

The curriculum framework, as previously noted, is one way in which blended programs can design, implement, and revise learning opportunities for groups and individual children. Within a curriculum framework, the "what is taught" is characterized by three tiers. At the bottom (the foundation), or what is often called tier 1, teachers are addressing common or universal outcomes that are often set forth by federal, state, and local agency standards. Examples of tier 1 outcomes for preschoolers include naming upper and lower case letters, developing motor control and balance when walking, running, and playing, and engaging in cooperative play with others. At tier 2, teachers are addressing outcomes for some children who may be struggling or for whom progress has stalled. Examples of tier 2 outcomes for preschoolers include gaining independence, performing tasks more quickly or with more control, and learning to initiate as well as to respond in order to get wants and needs met. At tier 3, teachers are addressing foundational or prerequisite skills a child may be missing, or barriers that are preventing the child from accessing, participating, and making progress toward the common outcomes. Examples of tier 3 outcomes for preschoolers include learning how to establish joint attention, understanding and using objects in representational ways, maintaining calm and focused emotional states, and imitating single word utterances. Tier 3 outcomes may also include critical or pivotal skills that at first glance appear to be an expectation for all children (a tier 1 outcome). However, in many cases, despite maturation and instruction children do not acquire basic skills that become the building blocks to more complex skills as they age. For example, if a child is nearing the end of pre-K and is unable to identify letters, he or she may experience difficulty with reading and writing in kindergarten and first grade. The skills of identifying letters, while something that was once a tier 1 outcome for all children, is elevated to a tier 3 need because an individual child did not acquire the skill as expected and requires more intensive instructional efforts.

Teachers need to have a clear sense of not only what they are teaching but what they are teaching all children, versus some children, versus an individual child.

Teachers in blended programs are responsible for delivering instruction across all three tiers of outcomes and, as much as possible, doing so within the same activity or routine. In other words, while in the block area, a teacher may encourage all children to learn about terms that describe the spatial relationship between objects/people (e.g., on, below, in front of, middle, near, far). At the same time, teach a few children who are struggling with spatial relations to be more accurate in identifying how objects are the same or different. Then, simultaneously, provide multiple opportunities for an individual child to better coordinate movement and vision as they explore the blocks and cars. Teachers need to have a clear sense of not only what they are teaching but what they are teaching all children, versus some children, versus an individual child.

Instructional Strategies

The instructional strategies used to teach across tiers need match the desired outcome. In other words, instructional strategies used to address tier 1 outcomes need to be effective and efficient for addressing these types outcomes; instructional strategies used at tier 2 need to be effective and efficient for addressing tier 2 types of outcomes, and so forth. This brings us to the second issue teachers face when working in a blended classroom, determining which instructional strategy is most effective and efficient for teaching which outcomes.

Instructional strategies can be placed on a continuum from low adult mediation/involvement to high adult mediation/involvement (Bredekamp & Rosegrant, 1995; Noonan & McCormick, 2014). Research has shown that outcomes focused more on child initiation are better matched with instructional strategies that require less adult mediation. Conversely, outcomes that are more focused on an individual child's response to a highly specific outcome are better matched with instructional strategies that require more adult mediation (Wolery & Wilbers, 1994). Thus, when teaching tier 1 *common* outcomes that are often focused on highly child initiated outcomes (e.g., counting objects, labeling the color of objects, problem solving), *universal* instructional strategies such as self-talk, environmental arrangement, and modeling can be used to ensure children's success. When teaching a subgroup of children who may be struggling with progressing toward tier 1 outcomes and, which are somewhat child initiated and somewhat adult specified (e.g., increasing response time when given directions), *targeted* instructional strategies such as differential reinforcement and small group instruction may be most effective (Grisham-Brown & Hemmeter, 2014). Finally, if a child is missing an adult-specified foundational/prerequisite skill or one that is preventing the child's access and participation, *intentional, intensive, individualized (III)* instructional strategies such as milieu teaching or response-prompting procedures might be needed (Odom & Wolery, 2003).

Unfortunately, while the implementation of III instructional strategies is necessary for ensuring progress toward tier 3 outcomes, they are not frequently used within blended classrooms. Odom (2009) shares a number of possible reasons why such instructional strategies, which do have a strong evidence base, may not be implemented on a regular basis. First, researchers who establish evidence base of III strategies often use well-controlled settings and highly structured procedures. Teachers in blended classrooms may feel unable to abide by the preciseness of the procedures described in the literature due to the competing demands of their classrooms, including overcrowding, adherence to multiple state and federal mandates, and the diverse learning needs of children. Second, the professional development provided to teachers in blended classrooms is often insufficient to ensure that they will implement III evidence-based strategies in their classrooms. Many teachers who work in blended classrooms have limited to no training early childhood special education (from where many III originate) and likely do not implement III instructional strategies because they have never heard of them or they received only a "one shot" workshop on their use. Therefore, additional training and support through coaching and communities of process should be available to increase the probability of implementation of III within blended classrooms.

The ability to identify multiple and varied outcomes (determining who needs to learn what) and matching those outcomes to a full continuum of instructional strategies (determining which strategies are efficient and effective) is at the heart of quality blended programming. Once these initial decisions are made, teachers must then find ways to ensure sufficient learning opportunities are provided to promote children's learning and development across tiered outcomes. As mentioned earlier, a research to practice gap that persists, particularly in blended classrooms, is the ability to deliver III instruction for children in context of play and other ongoing classroom activities where tier 1 and tier 2 outcomes are also being taught. The following section provides three illustrations of how children with tier 3 needs successfully received III instruction during daily activities and acquired their individualized outcomes when served in blended classrooms.

> *The ability to identify multiple and varied outcomes (determining who needs to learn what) and matching those outcomes to a full continuum of instructional strategies (determining which strategies are efficient and effective) is at the heart of quality blended programming.*

Success Stories

The set of instructional strategies described in the three scenarios have a strong evidence base for supporting learning for children with disabilities. Initial research, however, suggests a promise of their utility in blended classrooms (e.g., Grisham-Brown, Pretti-Frontczak, Hawkins, & Winchell, 2009; Grisham-Brown, Ridgley, Pretti-Frontczak, Litt, & Nielson, 2006) and their utility for any child being served, not just those with identified disabilities. The stories provided are shared directly from the early interventionists/teachers who worked daily with the children. The children included a child with autism, a child with challenging behaviors, and a kindergartener who was struggling, with the two latter children not being eligible for special education services but having intensive needs. In addition to illustrating the implementation of III, each of the scenarios shows how III was implemented in three different blended classrooms: a childcare center, a Head Start classroom, and a kindergarten classroom. For each child, we describe the individualized outcome, the context of delivery of III instruction, how the instruction was delivered, and the result.

Alice and Miguel

Alice was an early interventionist serving children in an urban area through visits to homes and community childcare centers. One of the children on Alice's caseload was Miguel, a 27-month-old boy who received early intervention services due to delays in cognitive and communication development. Miguel interacted well with other children and was easily motivated when engaged in child-directed play. He sometimes used single word utterances to get his wants and needs met but was inconsistent and often difficult to understand. Alice concluded that Miguel's limited verbal communication skills were keeping him from accessing and participating in the daily routine and that he needed III instruction to learn the foundational skill of saying/signing "more". Thus, Miguel's individualized outcome was to respond to directions, answer questions, or say/sign "more" to indicate when he needed or wanted "more" of something. Approximations were allowed.

After a brief Internet search and review of evidence-based strategies designed to promote communication skills, Alice selected the "mand model" procedure as an effective and efficient instructional strategy to teach Miguel how to request more (Christensen-Sandfort & Whinnery, 2011; Dinehart, Kaiser, & Hughes, 2009; Harjusola-Webb, & Robbins, 2012; Ingersoll, Meyer, Bonter, & Jelinek, 2012; Yoder, Molfese, & Gardnera, 2011). In general, the mand model procedure can be used when a child is learning words, learning to request, and/or learning to respond to questions (Noonan & McCormick, 2014). The basic premise of the strategy is for adults to give mands (e.g., give directions, make requests, ask questions, make statements) that require a verbal response from the child. Alice felt that this evidence-based strategy would be both effective and efficient for use with Miguel and in collaboration with the childcare staff decided to use the strategy during snack and free-play time.

Baseline data were collected for 2 days during snack and free play. During baseline (before Alice and the childcare staff started to use the mand model procedure), Miguel was given six opportunities (three during snack and three during free play) to say or sign "more." During baseline, he signed "more" only one time during snack. Because of Miguel's consistent nonresponding during baseline, Alice and staff decided to begin delivering the mand model procedure 10 times during snack and 10 times during free play. For example, during snack, a few goldfish were presented to Miguel. When he was finished eating the goldfish, Alice and the childcare staff waited to see if he would indicate the need for more by making an approximation or by signing or saying "more." Alice knew the opportunity was a match for using the mand model procedure because they waited until they had joint or mutual attention, which was on the empty plate. Then, when Miguel started looking from his plate to the box of goldfish crackers, a mand was delivered (i.e., Alice or the staff would say, "What do you want?" or "Say more"), and then would wait 3 seconds for Miguel to respond. If Miguel approximated or signed/said the word "more" after the mand, Alice affirmed by saying, "You want more crackers" and then gave him more crackers. If he did not sign or say "more" after 3 seconds, Alice or the staff modeled by signing or saying "more" and then gave Miguel more goldfish crackers if he modeled an approximation of the sign or word for "more." Following 4 days of III instruction during snack and free play, Miguel was signing or using the initial consonant ("m") following the mand, 8 of 10 opportunities during snack, and 10 of 10 opportunities during free play.

The results demonstrate the importance of selecting the appropriate instructional strategy and ensuring that a sufficient number of embedded learning opportunities are provided.

The results demonstrate the importance of selecting the appropriate instructional strategy and ensuring that a sufficient number of embedded learning opportunities are provided. Prior to implementing the III instruction, the teacher had tried simply modeling the correct response for Miguel. However, the consistent delivery of the mand model procedure was needed in order for the child to learn an important foundational communication skill of saying/signing "more".

Dot and James

Dot was a Head Start pre-K teacher in an urban area serving 20 children, including James, who was a 3-and-a-half-year-old boy. James had attended Head Start for 6 months. His development was on track in terms of verbal skills and was easily understood by his peers and other adults in the classroom. In addition, James's fine motor skills were a strength, as he could manipulate small toys, writing implements, and his toothbrush. Despite these strengths, James had clear challenges in his social development, although he did not have an identified social delay. Specifically, he struggled getting along with others during group activities and had difficulty attending to an activity for more than a few minutes. Additionally, while eating, he used his fingers to pick up food and put it in his mouth instead of using a fork or spoon. The expected social outcome for James was to *use utensils during mealtimes instead of eating with his fingers and hands.* While James had the fine motor ability to manipulate the utensils, eating food with his fingers was both socially unacceptable and unsanitary.

Peer-Mediated Intervention (PMI) was used to teach James to use utensils. Prior to the implementation of PMI, no other strategies had been implemented to assist him with learning the skill of using utensils. PMI is a strategy frequently used in inclusive center-based settings whereby a more competent peer models appropriate social or communication skills to a child who has delays in one of those developmental areas (Harris, Pretti-Frontczak, & Brown, 2009). Research supports the use of PMI to teach social skills and support friendships between children with social delays and their peers (Frea, Craig-Unkefer, Odom, & Johnson, 1999; Sperry, Neitzel, & Englhardt-Wells, 2010; Strain, Danko, & Kohler, 1995). Because of its effectiveness in teaching appropriate social behavior to young children with social delays, PMI was identified as a match for teaching James to use utensils appropriately.

Prior to implementing the instructional strategy, Jenna, a 4-and-a-half year old, was identified as the peer. Jenna had attended Head Start for 2 years and had mastered the target behavior (i.e., using eating utensils at mealtimes). As well, Jenna had excellent fine motor, cognitive, and language skills and was well liked by her peers. After she was identified, Jenna was taught how to implement the intervention using role play. Once Jenna was trained to deliver PMI, baseline data were collected for 3 days during breakfast and snack to verify that James did not use a utensil to feed himself. During this baseline phase, James did not use eating utensils to feed himself across the 3 days; rather he used his fingers/hands.

Following baseline, PMI was implemented. During each meal, a fork or spoon was provided and Jenna would sit next to James at the table to model how to use a fork or spoon to eat his food. Jenna followed the steps she learned, including establishing joint attention with James, and then giving him a verbal clue: "Use your fork/spoon to scoop up your food," and praising him if he did. If James attempted to scoop up his food, but did not get it on his fork/spoon, Jenna praised him for trying and showed him how to scoop it up and said, "hold the spoon like this." If James used his fingers to pick up the food, Jenna reminded him to use a spoon to scoop up the food and place it in his mouth by demonstrating and saying, "Watch me, this is how you scoop up the food and eat it." PMI was implemented for 3 weeks. James showed progress by the third day of instruction when he began using his eating utensils with reminders. By the end of the third week, James was using his utensils with only occasional reminders from Jenna and teachers.

This second scenario illustrates how an effective and efficient instructional strategy was delivered during ongoing classroom activities by capitalizing upon one of the strengths of a blended classroom—using peers to deliver the instruction. In the scenario, Jenna, as a more competent peer, helped to deliver III instruction to support another child who needed to learn how to demonstrate more socially appropriate skills during meals. In this way, Dot was able to simultaneously deliver tier 1 instruction to all the children and ensure multiple and varied learning opportunities for James to acquire his individualized outcome.

Cate and Kameron

Cate was a kindergarten teacher in an urban public school where the majority of the children lived in low-income family situations and many of the children were English Language Learners. One of Cate's children was Kameron, a 5-year-old who had been in kindergarten for 8 months and who did not have an identified delay. Kameron had not received out of the home or formal early care and education prior to kindergarten entry. Kameron's strengths included active engagement in learning, seeking help when needed, and working well during one-on-one activities. Throughout the school year, however, Kameron had difficulty in labeling upper and lower case letters of the English alphabet. Cate had implemented a variety of tier 1 and tier 2 instructional strategies to support Kameron in learning how to labeling letters including the use of hands-on materials, teaching in small groups, and scaffolding. However, as the end of the school year approached, Kameron could not consistently label letters, even those in her first name. Cate recognized that despite maturation and instruction Kameron was not acquiring the basic skill of letter identification. Because this skill serves as a building block to more complex literacy skills, Cate selected Kameron's tier 3 outcome as *to verbally label all seven letters in her first name.*

A progressive time delay procedure was then selected as the III to teach Kameron to label the letters in her first name. Progressive time delay (PTD) is characterized by a gradual delay interval, beginning at 0 second and increasing by 1 to 2 seconds, between the presentation of the task direction and the presentation of a prompt to support demonstration of the expected behavior (Walker, 2008). The procedure has been used to teach a variety of behaviors to young children with disabilities such as sight word identification (Casey, 2008), peer imitation (Wolery et al., 1993), and communication skills (Matson, Sevin, Box, Francis, & Sevin, 1993).

Baseline data were collected for 3 days, during a single 15-minute small group activity to verify that Kameron could not label upper and lower case letters in her first name. On one occurrence during baseline, Kameron identified the uppercase letter K, but that was the only letter before III was delivered. During instruction, Kameron participated in a small group activity lead by Cate and another small group activity lead by the teaching assistant. PTD was delivered over 10 school days where the adult provided manipulatives with the letters (K-A-M-E-R-O-N) listed on them, where Kameron was prompted to label each letter. On the first day of instruction, after asking Kameron to label a letter, the adult immediately and verbally modeled how to say the letter name. In essence, at 0 second time delay, all that Kameron was expected to do was to repeat the model provided by the adult. On the second day, the adult again asked Kameron to label a letter and waited 1 second before verbally modeling how to say the letter. The delay interval was increased by 1 second each day until the delay was 3 seconds between the request for Kameron to label a letter and the verbal model of the letter was provided. By the end of 10 days of III, Kameron was able to label all of the letters in her name (upper and lower case). PTD was subsequently used to teach a new set of letters during the remainder of the school year. With III, Kameron labeled all of the letters of the alphabet before the end of the year.

This scenario illustrates that PTD, while a strategy that has primarily been used to teach children with disabilities, shows promise for teaching children who do not have delays but who are having difficulty learning critical or pivotal skills. In other words, despite maturation and quality tier 1 instruction, select children served in blended classrooms may not acquire basic skills that become the building blocks to more complex skills as they age and may require III.

Summary

The purposes of this article were to describe two key practices associated with meeting the learning needs of children with diverse abilities served in blended center-based programs and to provide three illustrations of how children can successfully acquire individualized outcomes using a blended approach. While our stories do not demonstrate strict experimental control, or measure fidelity, each provides a glimpse into real classrooms where teachers are trying, on a daily basis, to address the challenges of working in blended programs.

From the work of these three teachers, two suggestions are offered for identifying outcomes and selecting instructional strategies. First, teachers need to have a strong understanding of developmental and learning trajectories that depict the interrelatedness of development, and the recognition that all children have needs that can be viewed as tiered or varied (i.e., at any particular time a child may exhibit strengths, may struggle, and may have intensive needs). This awareness allows for the delivery of III even for children who may not qualify for some form of specially designed instruction but do require intensive support. Second, teachers need to cull from the research, the recommended practices, and professional wisdom that has evolved for intervening and teaching children both with and without identified disabilities and delays. Pulling from both traditions gives teachers a greater number of effective and efficient instructional strategies that can be better matched with desired outcomes.

Through the journey of these three teachers, it became obvious that beyond determining what and how to teach, those working in blended classrooms need to remain grounded in the core principles of child development. Teachers need to fully understand how children's developmental status impacts the type of support provided (e.g., if a child is still a concrete learner, actual objects may be needed to convey information to a child) and have an awareness of the children interests and preferences to ensure that materials and activities are used to promote engagement. Finally, it is important for teachers to understand differences in children's abilities to process and act upon information. Prompts and cues must be delivered in a format that children can understand and in a consistent manner in order for any instructional strategy to be effective.

Emerging lessons about the realities of blended classrooms suggests that children with a wide range of abilities, including those with disabilities and those from culturally and linguistically different backgrounds may be successfully educated together. In fact, the three stories of Alice, Dot, and Cate specifically illustrate how children with intensive needs can be served in blended classrooms. Their stories demonstrate the success of carefully selecting evidence-based instructional strategies, systematically implementing those strategies, and relying on data-driven decision making to determine the attainment of important outcomes.

Note

For more information, please contact Jennifer Grisham-Brown at jgleat00@uky.edu

References

Bredekamp, S. & Rosegrant, T. (1995). *Reaching potentials: Transforming early childhood curriculum and assessment* (Vol. 2). Washington, DC: National Association for the Education of Young Children.

Casey, S. D. (2008). A comparison of within- and across- session progressive time delay procedures for teaching sight words to individuals with cognitive delays. *Behavior Analyst Today, 9* (3/4), 162-171.

Christensen-Sandfort, R. & Whinnery, S. B. (2011). Impact of milieu teaching on communication skills of young children with autism spectrum disorder. *Topics in Early Childhood Special Education, 32*(4), 211-222. doi:http://dx.doi.org/10.1177/0271121411404930

Dinehart, L. H. B., Kaiser, M. Y., & Hughes, C. R. (2009). Language delay and the effect of milieu teaching on children born cocaine exposed: A pilot study. *Journal of Developmental and Physical Disabilities, 21*(1), 9-22. Retrieved July 10, 2014, from http://ezproxy.uky.edu/login?url=http://search.proquest.com/docview/85687003?accountid=11836

Frea, W., Craig-Unkefer, L., Odom, S. L., & Johnson, D. (1999). Differential effects of structured social integration and group friendship activities for promoting social interaction with peers. *Journal of Early Intervention, 22*(3), 230-242.

Grisham-Brown, J. & Hemmeter, M. L. (2014). *Blended practices for teaching young children in inclusive settings* (2nd ed.). Manuscript in preparation.

Grisham-Brown, J. L., Hemmeter, M. L., & Pretti-Frontczak, K. (2005). *Blended Practices for Teaching Young Children in Inclusive Settings.* Baltimore: Brookes Publishing.

Grisham-Brown, J. & Pretti-Frontczak, K. (2011). *Assessing young children using blended practices.* Baltimore: Brookes Publishing.

Grisham-Brown, J. & Pretti-Frontczak, K. (2013). A curriculum framework for supporting young children served in blended programs. In V. Buysse and E. Peisner-Feinberg (Eds.). *Handbook of response to intervention (RtI) in early childhood.* Baltimore: Brookes Publishing.

Grisham-Brown, J. L., Pretti-Frontczak, K., Hawkins, S., & Winchell. B. (2009). An examination of how to address early learning standards for all children within blended preschool classrooms. *Topics in Early Childhood Special Education, 29*(3), 131-142.

Grisham-Brown, J. L., Ridgley, R., Pretti-Frontczak, K, Litt, C., & Nielson, A. (2006). Promoting positive learning outcomes for young children in inclusive classrooms: A preliminary study of children's progress toward pre-writing standards. *Journal of Intensive Behavior Intervention, 3*(1), 171-190.

Harjusola-Webb, S. & Robbins, S. H. (2012). The effects of teacher-implemented naturalistic intervention on the communication of preschoolers with autism. *Topics in Early Childhood Special Education, 32*(2), 99-110. doi:http://dx.doi.org/10.1177/0271121410397060

Harris, K. I., Pretti-Frontczak, K., & Brown, T. (2009). Peer-mediated intervention: An effective, inclusive strategy for all young children. *Young Children, 64*(2), 43-49.

Ingersoll, B., Meyer, K., Bonter, N., & Jelinek, S. (2012). A comparison of developmental social-pragmatic and naturalistic behavioral interventions on language use and social engagement in children with autism. *Journal of Speech, Language, and Hearing Research, 55*(5), 1301-1313. Retrieved July 10, 2014, from http://ezproxy.uky.edu/login?url=http://search.proquest.com/docview/1315888852?accountid=11836

Matson, J. L., Sevin, J. A., Box, M. L., Francis, K. L., & Sevin, B. M. (1993). An evaluation of two methods for increasing self initiated verbalizations in autistic children. *Journal of Applied Behavior Analysis, 26*(3), 389–398.

Noonan, M. J. & McCormick (2014). *Teaching young children with disabilities in natural environments.* Baltimore: Brookes Publishing.

Odom, S. (2009). Evidence-based practice, implementation science, and outcomes for children (2009). *Topics in Early Childhood Special Education, 29*(53), 53-61.

Odom, S. & Wolery, M. (2003). A unified theory of practice in early intervention/early childhood special education: Evidence based practices. *Journal in Special Education, 37*(3), 164-173.

Sperry, L., Neltzel, J., & Englhardt-Wells, K. (2010). Peer involvement and intervention strategies for students with autism spectrum disorders. *Prevention of School Failure, 54*(4), 256-264.

Strain, P. S., Danko, C. D., & Kohler, P. (1995). Activity engagement and social interaction development in young children with autism: An examination of "free" intervention effects. *Journal of Emotional and Behavioral Disorders, 3*(2), 108-123.

Walker, G. (2008). Constant and progressive time delay procedures for teaching children with autism: A literature review. *Journal of Autism and Developmental Disorders, 38*(2), 261-275.

Wolery, M., Holcombe-Ligon, A., Brookfield, J., Huffman, K., Schroeder, C., Martin, C. G., Fleming, L. A. (1993). The extent and nature of preschool mainstreaming. A survey of general early educators. *Journal of Special Education, 27*(2), 222-234. doi:http://dx.doi.org/10.1177/002246699302700205

Wolery, M. & Wilbers, J. S. (1994). Introduction to the inclusion of young children with special needs in early childhood programs. In M. Wolery & J. S. Wilbers (Eds.), *Including children with special needs in early childhood programs* (pp. 1-22). Washington, DC: National Association for the Education of Young Children.

Yoder P., Molfese, D., & Gardner, E. (2011). Initial mean length of utterance predicts the relative efficacy of two grammatical treatments in preschoolers with specific language impairment. *Journal of Speech, Language, and Hearing Research, 54*(4), 1170–81.

From All to Each and Every: Preparing Professionals to Support Children of Diverse Abilities

Camille Catlett, M.A.,
Frank Porter Graham Child Development Institute

Susan P. Maude, Ph.D.,
Iowa State University

Melanie Nollsch, M.S., and Susan Simon, M.A.,
Kirkwood Community College

Why would my students need to know about assistive technology? That's just for special education students.

Question posed by an early childhood faculty member from Ohio,
January 2014

Over a decade of research has consistently revealed the lack of emphasis on young children of diverse abilities in the coursework and field experiences of associate's and bachelor's degree programs that are preparing early childhood teachers (Chang, Early, & Winton, 2005; Goor & Porter, 1999; Maude et al., 2010; Maxwell, Lim, & Early, 2006; Ray, Bowman, & Robbins, 2006). Thus, it is not surprising when a national study reveals that while 71% of surveyed teachers taught students with disabilities, only about 17% felt very well prepared to meet the needs of these students (National Center for Education Statistics, 2002). As well documented as preparation shortcomings are, both internal and external constraints (e.g., lack of philosophical support from upper administration, reliance on adjuncts, lack of professional development for faculty members vis-à-vis new content or priorities) make changes in emphasis in preservice early childhood programs difficult (Hyson, Tomlinson, & Morris, 2009).

In many ways, early childhood educators are the gatekeepers of opportunities for young children of diverse abilities to fully participate in learning, development, and play with typically developing peers. It is within their classrooms, with appropriate services, supports, and collaboration, that young children of diverse abilities enjoy the full benefits of quality inclusion. Fueled by recent revisions in standards (National Association for the Education of Young Children, 2009a), position statements (Division for Early Childhood/National Association for the Education of Young Children, 2009), and evidence-based practices (National Professional Development Center on Inclusion, 2011), support by families and professionals for quality inclusion is higher than ever.

This article highlights how one early childhood associate degree program set out to more effectively prepare future early childhood educators to support young children of diverse abilities in inclusive settings. The lessons learned from this project can help others realign their priorities for, and perspectives on, supporting each young child, whether by preparing future professionals, delivering training and technical assistance, or working directly to support children and families.

Setting the Stage

In 2010, Kirkwood Community College in Cedar Rapids, Iowa, with support from a grant from the Office of Special Education Programs, set out to examine and revise their paraeducator program in early childhood education to better support young children who are culturally, linguistically, and/or ability diverse. Kirkwood's Associate of Applied Science (AAS) in Early Childhood Education (ECE) is a sequence of preparation that requires nine early childhood education courses, plus four or five additional courses in early childhood and/or special education.[1] The federal grant required program leaders at Kirkwood to examine and revise required courses to incorporate an emphasis on 11 areas of evidence-based practice for supporting young children of diverse abilities in early childhood settings (see Figure 1). In addition, program leaders were tasked with incorporating field experiences that would prepare students to support diverse young learners and providing professional development that would prepare faculty to fully incorporate new methods, models, and materials in their coursework.

To support the sequence of change and improvement required by the grant, the early childhood leaders at Kirkwood Community College used an evidence-based model for supporting change in higher education programs called the Crosswalks Intervention Model as the basis for

---

[1] It is important to note that the AAS in Early Childhood program at Kirkwood Community College was a very strong program before applying for the grant. Leaders at this institution have been actively and successfully working to grow the quality of the program for many years. Application for, and perseverance through, this project show the extent to which this program is committed to quality and excellence.

Figure 1

Areas of Evidence-Based Practice Required by the Office of Special Education Programs (OSEP)

1.	Knowledge of typical disability conditions
2.	Expectations and outcomes related to children of diverse abilities
3.	Instructional strategies to support early development and learning, or preacademic achievement
4.	Skills for modifying learning environments to meet the needs of young children of diverse abilities
5.	Skills for observation and data collection
6.	Skills for assisting in the implementation of transition plans and services across settings
7.	Skills for communicating effectively with children and families
8.	Skills for developing and implementing IFSPs and IEPs
9.	Skills for providing clear expectations for outcomes of children who are culturally and linguistically diverse and their families
10.	Skills for emphasizing social-emotional and behavioral interventions and classroom management practices
11.	Skills for collaborating and working effectively with related services professionals/practitioners

enhancing coursework and developing instructor expertise (Maude et al., 2010). Where the original Crosswalks Intervention Model addressed change and improvement related to incorporating cultural and linguistic diversity, Kirkwood's adaptation of the Crosswalks model used the same five-step framework to incorporate an emphasis on ability diversity, while at the same time paying attention to ways in which cultural and linguistic diversity could also be infused.

What Did We Do?

Kirkwood's approach unfolded in the same five phases as were used in the Crosswalks Intervention Model (see Figure 2). In the *first phase* of the 4-year project, Kirkwood leaders formed an Advisory Committee consisting of full-time and adjunct faculty members, and community partners drawn from Head Start, local schools, the Area Education Agency, graduates of the Kirkwood program working in the early childhood field, and faculty from related disciplines. Early in the project, a full-day retreat with key Kirkwood faculty, adjuncts, and community partners provided an opportunity to develop a shared vision of

Figure 2
Phases of Kirkwood Project Approach

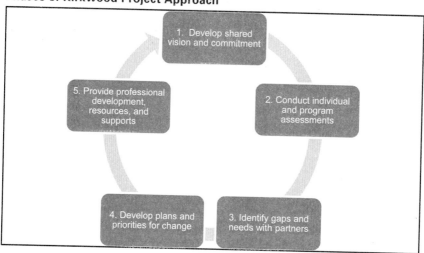

the knowledge, skills, and dispositions they wanted to grow in each graduate of the program. This was accomplished through a Crosswalks Intervention activity called the Graduate of the Future, which invited faculty members and community partners to collaboratively develop a picture of what they wanted future graduates of the early childhood program to know and be able to do.

The *second phase* of the process, focused on gathering information about all components of the Kirkwood early childhood program through a systematic needs assessment process. Information about the program, the faculty members, and the students were each assessed in a variety of ways, as described below. Please note that these are only a partial listing of the needs assessments, faculty, student, and/or program measures that were used.

- Three aspects of the overall early childhood program—coursework, field experiences, and program practices—were assessed by faculty members and community partners. Individuals were asked to identify areas of strength and areas for improvement, all of which were then compiled in a profile of the program.
- Information about the knowledge, skills, and capabilities of Kirkwood faculty members were assessed using the Crosswalks Assessment of Knowledge, Skills, and Instructional Strategies (CAKSkIS).
- Each Kirkwood syllabus was assessed using a rubric organized by areas required by the OSEP grant (see Figure 1). In addition to review by faculty and advisory committee members, syllabi were also reviewed by independent outside evaluators.

The *third phase* provided the opportunity to examine all findings using data from evaluations and input from the retreat. Attention was paid to areas in which instructors showed less content expertise and to aspects of content that were not reflected in course syllabi. With these data in hand, plans were developed for ways in which to build capability (the *fourth phase*). Different approaches were identified based on the nature of the finding (e.g., one-on-one consultation, whole group presentation). With plans and priorities articulated, the work of the *fifth phase*—the provision of professional development, resources, and supports to achieve targeted changes—could unfold. Examples that follow will highlight changes in two major components of the associate degree program: (1) course syllabi and (2) knowledge and skill of faculty members and community partners. Diversity of knowledge and skill across participants was taken into account in designing professional development. For example, all adjunct faculty, some community partners, and Kirkwood's program leaders hold master's degrees in either early childhood or special education. Other community partners held associate degrees in early childhood. The roles or agencies represented as "community partners" also reflected those serving on the advisory board (Head Start, community child care, Area Education Agency, paraeducators, school district teachers, etc.).

To address priorities for changes in course syllabi, Kirkwood colleagues used a process from the Crosswalks Intervention (deconstruction/reconstruction). Each of the eight syllabi was reviewed by an outside content expert who suggested evidence-based sources, readings, audiovisual materials, and Web sites for incorporating the desired areas of emphasis. Possible revisions to activities and assignments were also offered. The Kirkwood program director worked with the adjunct faculty members who teach each course to revise all aspects of the syllabus. The outside content expert reviewed the revised syllabi and offered additional suggestions. Then, after additional revisions and over time, each syllabus was reassessed using the syllabus rubric to measure progress by both the participating faculty members and an external evaluator. A summary of that progress is displayed in Figure 3.

One starting point for the revisions was to make certain that language used in each syllabus was inclusive and explicit. For example, faculty members shifted from using the word *parents* to either *family* or *parents and family*. This explicit and consistent change was a constant reminder to faculty and students alike that the broader term was inclusive of people such as aunts, grandmothers, siblings, foster families, and others in each child's life. This also took the form of introducing new terms and content. For many of the early childhood faculty members, for example, assistive technology was a relatively unfamiliar concept. When resources and

Figure 3

Course Syllabi Rubric Scoring Results by External Evaluator, Results Are Reflective of Syllabi from 2008 to 2013.

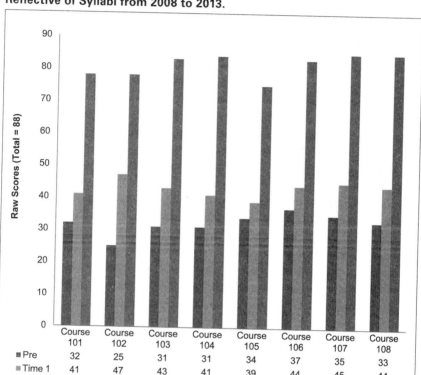

	Course 101	Course 102	Course 103	Course 104	Course 105	Course 106	Course 107	Course 108
■ Pre	32	25	31	31	34	37	35	33
■ Time 1	41	47	43	41	39	44	45	44
■ Time 2	78	78	83	84	75	83	85	85

Kirkwood Community College - Heartland Early Childhood Courses

ideas for how to use assistive technology to support the full participation of children with and without disabilities were shared, faculty readily embraced the shift and identified ways to incorporate an emphasis on assistive technology in each Kirkwood course.

Another starting point was to identify and incorporate evidence-based practices that were underpinnings for each course, drawing on resources from the National Association for the Education of Young Children (NAEYC) and the Division for Early Childhood of the Council for Exceptional Children (DEC/CEC), among others. This supported the priority for all changes to Kirkwood syllabi to support alignment with both national (DEC, NAEYC) and state standards.

Support for growth in faculty and community partner expertise took several forms. Professional development sessions were organized around content areas that were targeted for enhancement from the initial knowledge, skills, and instructional strategies survey as well as what emerged in discussion or end-of-session evaluation forms during ongoing professional development activities. Some sessions were organized exclusively for faculty and incorporated examples of how new content could be addressed through readings, activities, and assignments. Other sessions provided rich opportunities for faculty and community partners to learn together. For example, one area for enhancement was building the capacity of students to respond to dilemmas in their daily practice (e.g., incorporating Individualized Education Program (IEP) goals for one child embedded within the daily early childhood curriculum). To prepare for the professional development on this topic, faculty gathered examples of dilemmas that frequently arise in settings that support young children of diverse abilities. Presenters then shared effective approaches for navigating real world dilemmas. The result enabled faculty to incorporate the dilemmas and the approaches in their coursework and collaborate with community partners to implement or share the same approaches.

To ensure that new areas of emphasis were not superficial (e.g., one new article), Kirkwood developed a tool they call a curriculum map. Curriculum maps were designed to ensure that key concepts were embedded in all early childhood courses in ways that built knowledge and skill without being repetitive. So, for example, the curriculum map on inclusion identifies specific media, speakers, materials, instructional approaches, and assignments that can be used to increase the emphasis on inclusion in *each* course in the Kirkwood program. (Note: Kirkwood's curriculum maps are available to view or download at the early childhood program's Web site.) Additional strategies for developing expertise included purchasing resources and software especially in the area of assistive technology (e.g., Boardmaker™).

What Happened?

The instrument used to evaluate the eight syllabi consisted of a 22-item rubric organized across the following areas: Course Description (four items); Course Objectives (five items); Texts, Readings, and Resources (three items); Assignments (five items); Guest Speakers (two items); and In-Class Instructional Experiences (three items). Individual indicators under each of the six areas included statements assessing whether there was evidence of cultural diversity, linguistic diversity, ability diversity,

I think the vocabulary (diversity, problem solving, adaptations) we have been using has become more universal in all of the classes, too.

Faculty member

evidence-based practices, problem solving, and/or collaboration in the syllabus and supporting documents. The rating scale ranged from 1 or None/Little, 2 or Some, 3 or Significantly, to 4 or Extensively. The maximum score possible was 88. Kirkwood's target was a score of 70 or higher on each syllabus.

Syllabi were evaluated across multiple time periods (pre-intervention or baseline, Time 1, and Time 2). Data were shared with key faculty members and adjunct staff at each point in time so professional development could be focused on areas in which growth was not occurring. For instance, syllabi were showing little growth in the areas of problem solving so a focused professional development retreat was designed on the use of cultural dilemmas as an instructional strategy supporting problem solving and diversity.

Figure 3 provides a summary of the results obtained by the external evaluator. Here you can see some growth between the pre- or baseline syllabi and Time 1 (1 year after the scoring of pre-syllabi) with significant growth at Time 2 (two years after scoring the Time 1 syllabi). Although not all syllabi were able to obtain the maximum score of 88, all demonstrated significant growth and improvement over time, having received low initial scores between 25 and 37 and moving to higher, more positive scores ranging from 75 to 85. All syllabi exceeded the target goal of 70 points or higher.

Multiple measures and methods were used to capture changes in faculty members and community partners' knowledge, skills, and dispositions. These included self-assessment instruments (pre-/post-), end of professional development retreat or event evaluations, and focus groups. At this time we are able to share these additional results obtained from the following: (1) end of retreat surveys by faculty members and community partners and (2) focus group data from full-time and adjunct faculty members and students. Capturing change in professional development has some limitations when using a traditional pretest-posttest model of evaluation.

The directions are much clearer, and we have definitely put an emphasis on adaptations for all of the activities in the course assignments.

Kirkwood student

Often participants do not "know what they don't know" until after the professional development activities are conducted. Therefore, we chose to implement a retrospective pretest model (Allen & Nimon, 2007; Lynch, 2002) at various points across the project in addition to traditional pretest-posttest methods. In a retrospective pretest model

Figure 4
Evaluation of Professional Development Events by Faculty

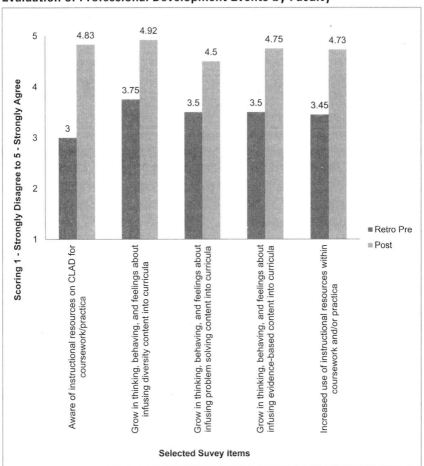

Selected Suvey Items

one collects both pretest and posttest evaluation data at the end of the professional development activity.

Typically, participants are asked to rate their perceptions on their knowledge, skills, or dispositions after the event and compare that to where they would rate themselves prior to the professional development event. As noted in Figure 4, faculty members and community partners indicated positive shifts in their awareness, growth in reflecting about, and/or use of instructional strategies that supported infusion of culture, language, and/or ability diversity. These data were further supported as we collected more qualitative data.

A series of focus groups were facilitated by both the internal and external evaluators. Students participated in a focus group as they were exiting their program while full-time and adjunct faculty members participated in one of two focus groups held approximately half-way through the grant cycle. The feedback from faculty members identified several themes that underscore progress on the targeted goals. First, they reported an increased understanding of expectations for them on specific curricular and content areas to be covered in their course work.

Second, faculty members indicated that they were exposed to and willing to utilize evidence-based resources on culture, language, and ability diversity within their coursework. As one faculty member said,

> *Just knowing that these resources are out there is new—especially the Web sites [for OSEP-funded projects]. For instance, the professional sites like CSEFEL [the Center on the Social and Emotional Foundations of Early Learning]... just being able to refer to the articles and pull those research-based articles to support what's already (covered) in the text.*

Third, faculty members identified an increased awareness about and emphasis on culture, language, or ability diversity across the ECE curriculum as a whole. One faculty member offered this example:

> *I was teaching about how you can teach children to write and all that is involved. ... I noticed that in my class of 10 students that night a third of them were English language learners themselves. I asked to be sure there weren't any others, and I never would have done that before. But the three that were English language learners, one was Spanish, one was Chinese, and one was Hindi. So I had them each come up and write their name, in their (home) language, their native language on the chalkboard. Then they each shared their stories about how each of them learned English, and they were all a little bit different.*

When asked specifically if they would have done any of the previous activities before this grant, a typical response was

> *I really don't think so. I never have [done that] and I've taught that class session many times before. It was just that awareness [that I have gained through the grant] of cultural differences and language learning that brought it to my mind. I didn't plan it in advance. You know it was just something that I was aware of as we were talking about the topic of how we teach writing.*

Finally, faculty members shared how participating on this grant made them more intentional in addressing culture, language, and ability diversity. As one said,

*I'm reflecting more and I practice (strategies more). I'm think-
ing a lot more about what I've done each evening after I teach.
I used to not really think that much about it actually but I
really think now and I'm trying a little bit differently because
I'm always thinking about the Heartland Grant and how can
I incorporate some aspects of it [what I've learned] each time
I'm teaching.*

Lessons for All

The lessons from this project have implications for all the participating
partners (faculty members, professional development providers, early
childhood special education and allied health colleagues, and early childhood practitioners). For faculty, the most obvious lesson learned is that
the Crosswalks Intervention was very effective in supporting desired
changes in course syllabi related to increased emphasis on evidence-
based practices for supporting diverse young learners. Even though data
analysis is not complete, Kirkwood has also learned that the Crosswalks
Intervention has supported many desired changes in the knowledge and
skill of faculty members.

Additional lessons reflect benefits directly to the Kirkwood program,
to the community, and to other institutions of higher education in the
state. Benefits to the program included the alignment of ongoing professional development with areas of strength and need. For example, lower
CAKSkIS scores on content related to supporting dual language learners,
with and without disabilities, and their families led to a sequence of workshops and resources on that topic. Because professional development was
provided for both faculty members and community partners, another
positive outcome was increased capacity to use evidence-based practices
for serving young dual language learners in community field experience
sites.

Additional benefits for participating community partners included
expanded familiarity with the ECE program at Kirkwood, as well as a
stronger sense of investment in, commitment to, and ownership of the
program. For example, when Kirkwood faculty members visited community sites, they incorporated real dilemmas that early childhood teachers encounter in their teaching; community partners were impressed
with that effort to "keep it real." In addition, opportunities for faculty
members and community partners to participate in professional development together heightened both the common knowledge of topics such
as inclusion and the shared commitment to preparing students, through
the integration of course work and field experiences, to support progress

Because it is incorporated in all of the courses, we're seeing it in the students as they come through our courses, and we're seeing it then in their practice. When they're doing their field experience and when they're doing their lesson planning.

Faculty member

on their shared vision of a Graduate of the Future. In addition, a shared vocabulary has also built the capacity for communication and collaboration across early childhood and early childhood special education partners.

The other lesson learned through this process has been that change takes time and commitment, a burden made lighter by shared commitment and participation. In Kirkwood's case, the initial investment (Phases 1–5) took over 2 years. The commitment to continued self-assessment and change by this program will ensure that the investments in time and energy will reap rewards for their students, community partners, and the children and families served.

While the level of support, commitment, and change that Kirkwood brought to the change process would be difficult to accomplish without external support, there are lessons they learned that could be of use to any program. Here are six ideas for ways to tackle some of the tasks they accomplished:

1. *Be explicit* with the words, images, and examples you use. Develop an inclusive vocabulary and an intentional filter and use them consistently to examine everything you produce.

2. *Establish a clear vision* for what you want your students or staff to know and be able to do. Using an activity like Graduate of the Future (or a teacher or early interventionist of the future) would be one way. Once a program is clear about the attributes they want each student or staff member to achieve, it will support decisions about what's important and what's not. Further, a clear vision will enable a program to frequently reassess progress toward achieving their vision.

3. *Become skilled* at using approaches that build the capacity for early childhood settings to support children of diverse abilities. For example, Universal Design for Learning (UDL) is a set of practices that help teachers, therapists, and administrators to design and implement early care and education environments that remove physical and structural barriers and provides multiple and varied formats for instruction and learning. The revised DEC Recommended Practices

(Division for Early Childhood, 2014) highlight the effectiveness of UDL (e.g., E2. Practitioners consider Universal Design for Learning principles to create accessible environments).

4. *Use sources from other fields.* Participants in this process benefited tremendously from increased access to evidence-based sources and materials from other fields. Early childhood special education colleagues became more familiar with the emphasis in individually appropriate practice that is foundational to NAEYC's position statement on developmentally appropriate practice (National Association for the Education of Young Children, 2009b). Similarly, early childhood colleagues became more familiar with DEC's Recommended Practices (Division for Early Childhood, 2014).

5. *Embrace resources that bridge diverse fields and perspectives.* The DEC-NAEYC joint position on inclusion is a good example of a resource that can provide a connection among diverse colleagues who want to blend their efforts to support each child's full potential (Division for Early Childhood/National Association for the Education of Young Children, 2009). Or, the Supporting Change and Reform in Preservice Training Project (SCRIPT-NC) has developed "landing pads" of resources for increasing the emphasis on cultural, linguistic, and ability diversity in college courses. Landing pads are available at the project's Web site from which anyone can download resources nine different early childhood topics (http://scriptnc.fpg.unc.edu/resource-search). While these materials were originally developed to share resources that support cultural, linguistic, and ability diversity with faculty members, they are also collections on which students, practitioners, administrators, or family members can draw for evidence-based sources, audiovisual materials, or Web sites.

6. *Establish a community of practice* of faculty members, community partners, and family members to support ongoing program improvements. Be sure to include recent graduates because they will be able to candidly describe what they learned that has been helpful and what they didn't learn but really needed.

The work at Kirkwood Community College provides a powerful model of how one program can support the shift from preparing students to work with *all* children to preparing them to support *each* and *every* child and family. How will you use the lessons they learned to make your own work more explicit, intentional, and inclusive?

Note
For more information, please contact Camille Catlett at camille.catlett@unc.edu

References

Allen, J. M. & Nimon, K. (2007). Retrospective pretest: A practical technique for professional development evaluation. *Journal of Industrial Teacher Education, 44*(3), 27-42.

Chang, F., Early, D., & Winton, P. (2005). Early childhood teacher preparation in special education at 2- and 4-year institutions of higher education. *Journal of Early Intervention, 27*(2), 110-124.

Division for Early Childhood. (2014). DEC recommended practices in early intervention/early childhood special education. Los Angeles: Author. Retrieved on July 15, 2014 from http://www.dec-sped.org/recommendedpractices

Division for Early Childhood/National Association for the Education of Young Children. (2009). *Early childhood inclusion: A joint position statement of the Division for Early Childhood (DEC) and the National Association for the Education of Young Children (NAEYC)*. Chapel Hill: University of North Carolina and FPG Child Development Institute. Retrieved on July 15, 2014 from http://npdci.fpg.unc.edu/resources/articles/Early_Childhood_Inclusion

Goor, M. B. & Porter, M. (1999). Preparation of teachers and administrators for working effectively with multicultural students. In F. E. Obiakor, J. O. Schwenn, & A. F. Rotatori (Eds.), *Advances in special education* (pp. 183-204). Stamford, CT: JAI Press.

Hyson, M., Tomlinson, H. B., & Morris, C. (2009). Quality improvement in early childhood teacher education: Faculty perspectives and recommendations for the future. *Early Childhood Research & Practice, 11*(1). Retrieved on July 15, 2014 from http://ecrp.uiuc.edu/v11n1/hyson.html

Lynch, K. B. (2002, November). *When you don't know what you don't know: Evaluating workshops and training sessions using the retrospective pretest methods.* Paper presented at the meeting of the American Evaluation Association Annual Conference, Arlington, VA.

Maude, S. P., Catlett, C., Moore, S., Sánchez, S. Y., Thorp, E., & Corso, R. (2010). Infusing diversity constructs in preservice teacher preparation: The impact of a systematic faculty development strategy. *Infants and Young Children, 23*(2), 1-19.

Maxwell, K. L., Lim, C.-I., & Early, D. M. (2006). *Early childhood teacher preparation programs in the United States: National report.* Chapel Hill: University of North Carolina, FPG Child Development Institute.

National Association for the Education of Young Children. (2009a). Standards for early childhood professional preparation. Washington, DC: Author. Retrieved on July 15, 2014 from http://www.naeyc.org/files/naeyc/files/2009%20Professional%20Prep%20stdsRevised%204_12.pdf

National Association for the Education of Young Children. (2009b). Developmentally appropriate practice in early childhood programs serving children from birth through age 8. Washington, DC: Author. Retrieved on July 15, 2014 from https://www.naeyc.org/files/naeyc/file/positions/PSDAP.pdf

National Center for Education Statistics. (2002). *The condition of education 2002.* Washington: GPO.

National Professional Development Center on Inclusion. (2011). *Research synthesis points on practices that support inclusion.* Chapel Hill: University of North Carolina, FPG Child Development Institute, Author. Retrieved on July 15, 2014 from http://npdci.fpg.unc.edu/sites/npdci.fpg.unc.edu/files/resources/NPDCI-ResearchSynthesisPointsInclusivePractices-2011_0.pdf

Ray, A., Bowman, B., & Robbins, J. (2006). Preparing early childhood teachers to successfully educate all children: The contribution of four-year undergraduate teacher preparation programs. Report to The Foundation for Child Development. Chicago: Erikson Institute. Retrieved on July 14, 2014 from http://www.erikson.edu/wp-content/uploads/Teachered.pdf

Infant/Toddler Professional Preparation and Development Using Blended Practices and Tiered Supports

Adam S. Kennedy, Ph.D.,

Anna T. Lees, M.A.,
Loyola University Chicago

Research on tiered models of service delivery in early childhood is limited; this is particularly true for infants and toddlers, as nearly all research on such models in early childhood has focused on preschool-aged children (Greenwood et al., 2011). Professional development for infant-toddler professionals regarding data-based decision making within multitiered systems of support (MTSS) is also a research area in need of expansion (Division for Early Childhood [DEC], National Association for the Education of Young Children [NAEYC], & National Head Start Association [NHSA], 2013). While Early Head Start (EHS) has not been extensively examined as a context for tiered models, EHS centers have provided us with what is in many ways an ideal setting for considering MTSS. This article explores some of the ways in which the professional preparation of early childhood educators and the professional development of EHS teachers may be merged through a focus on blended practices and tiered models. Specifically, by refocusing early childhood teacher education and professional development through the lens of partnership between EHS teachers, university faculty, and early childhood teacher candidates, university-based and center-based partners can support one another's work toward the shared goals of learning and enhancing blended practices, facilitating a deeper understanding of tiered models, and combining resources to promote the development of infants/toddlers and their families.

In this article, we define blended practices as those that support infant and toddler development in inclusive settings, specifically by aligning developmentally appropriate practice (DAP) and best practices for children with special needs (Grisham-Brown, Hemmeter, & Pretti-Frontczak, 2005). We present an example of blended practices in EHS with university faculty, EHS teachers, and undergraduate early childhood special education (ECSE) teacher candidates working together to achieve the following interconnected goals: (1) building awareness of diverse individual needs in the EHS classroom; (2) supporting teacher candidates to provide access to and include *all* infants and toddlers in activity, assessment, and intervention planning; and (3) supporting EHS teachers in critically examining their curriculum to ensure that it provides access for infants and toddlers at every ability level. We share this model as an example of how field-based, birth-to-three teacher preparation can and should provide benefits for both practicing and future teachers.

> *By refocusing early childhood teacher education and professional development through the lens of partnership, university-based and center-based educators can support one another's work*

MTSS complement this process and serve as an essential element of blending. These systems expand beyond serving children with identified needs, including all children in practices that rely upon data-based decision making for the planning and delivery of supportive practices at intensity levels that are matched to children's needs. Tiered models require collaborative teams to sustain them, and developing this collaboration is a complex undertaking and not a discrete event. The information shared in this article focuses primarily on the integration of multitiered systems into the preparation of teacher candidates and the professional development of EHS teachers (Winton, 2013). The strategies discussed here have been successfully implemented within one university-EHS partnership, which will be described in the next sections.

> *Field-based birth-to-three teacher preparation can and should provide benefits for both practicing and future teachers*

The Current Context Supports Collaborative Field-Based Teacher Education

Teacher education is undergoing a transformation from university-based coursework to collaborative field-based experiences, which provide teacher candidates with opportunities to practice their skills in authentic contexts (American Association of Colleges of Teacher Education [AACTE], 2010; Darling-Hammond & Baratz-Snowden, 2007; Lim & Able-Boone, 2005; National Council for Accreditation of Teacher Education [NCATE], 2011; Rust, 2010). However, developing effective teachers involves more than simply increasing field hours; it requires new roles of university faculty and practicing educators, as well as an emphasis on practices that support not only candidates but the teachers who mentor them as well (NAEYC, 2009; NCATE, 2011).

Teaching, Learning, and Leading with Schools and Communities (TLLSC) is an urban, field-based undergraduate ECSE teacher education program designed as a response to this call for change. TLLSC is an example of a preparation program anchored in collaboration between university and school/community organizations to prepare all ECSE teachers to work specifically in blended classrooms with children from birth to eight (Kennedy & Heineke, 2014). TLLSC was developed through collaboration with community partners (including an EHS agency) to simultaneously address another critical need: to enhance professional development options for early childhood educators and re-envision teacher education and professional development as part of a single transactional partnership between a university and community agency/school (Kruger, T., & Teaching Australia - Australian Institute for Teaching and School Leadership, 2009). Building beyond a professional development school (PDS) model (Darling-Hammond, 1994), which focuses primarily on 1-year student teaching internships, TLLSC embeds teacher candidates in field-based learning throughout all 4 years of their preparation.

Developing effective teachers involves more than simply increasing field hours; it requires new roles of university faculty and practicing educators

University faculty, EHS teachers, and teacher candidates partner in semester-long sequences to develop candidates' and classrooms teachers' skills in tiered models within blended classrooms. The themes, strategies, and reflections offered in this article are products of the implementation of a semester-long birth-to-three sequence in which coursework and clinicals were replaced with a TLLSC sequence co-led with EHS partners. This sequence emphasized culturally responsive and DAP with infants/toddlers and families, and introduced blended and tiered practices as well.

Figure 1
Pathways for Merging Teacher Education and Professional Development in Infant-Toddler Settings (Kennedy & Heineke, 2014)

MERGING EARLY CHILDHOOD PREPARATION AND PROFESSIONAL DEVELOPMENT TO SUPPORT BLENDED PRACTICE AND TIERED SUPPORTS		
TRADITIONAL APPROACH		**COLLABORATIVE, COMMUNITY-BASED PREPARATION WITH BLENDED PROGRAMS**
Preparation takes place at the university, followed by clinical experiences and later professional development that may or may not support learned practices.	APPROACH	Faculty and teacher candidates are embedded in blended community programs, developing practices through an apprenticeship model.
A static model compartmentalizes coursework, clinical experiences, and the continued development of practicing teachers.	FRAMEWORK	A reflexive model aimed at responsiveness to the needs of diverse children and families (in birth-to-three settngs) better reflects the complexity of teaching.
Separating the roles of teacher and researcher reinforces the research-practice gap and school-university divide.	RESEARCH TO PRACTICE	Teacher candidates and teachers learn and implement evidence-based approaches while generating practice-based evidence of their effectiveness.
Clinical supervisors form a link between university-based faculty and cooperating teachers.	STAKEHOLDERS	University faculty form collaborative relationships with infant/toddler programs and facilitate on-site work within communities.
Teachers host candidates/follow university guidelines and seek their own professional development.	PARTNERS	Partners serve as co-teacher educators and members of transactional feedback system for blended practices in the classroom.
Faculty lead university-based courses covering blended practices and multi-tiered systems of support.	FACULTY ROLES	Faculty provide PD and model/support blended practices and tiered supports with infants/toddlers and teacher candidates.
Candidates accumulate knowledge in courses for later application in clinical settings.	TEACHER CANDIDATES	From day one, candidates embody inclusive practice and plan to meet the needs of groups and individuals—both typically developing and those with special needs.
Teacher preparation is successful when graduates pass certification examinations and are retained in professional settings.	DEFINITION OF SUCCESS	Candidates are continuously evaluated on a growth model in blended B-8 settings, eventually entering the field having already made a measurable impact on children and families.

Pathways toward the Achievement of Shared Goals in Early Head Start

Figure 1 displays eight of the ways early childhood teacher education partnerships can be shifted from more traditional, segregated, place-ment-based approaches (on the left of each row) to more collaborative partnerships that support blended practices and tiered models on the right.

Rather than learning about these practices at the university and applying that knowledge later in clinicals and student teaching, candidates more effectively master teaching by learning alongside practicing professionals through guided apprenticeship (Lim & Able-Boone, 2005; McDonald et al., 2011). This allows for both teacher education *and* the continued development of professionals to occur within the contexts of early childhood education (ECE): school, center, community, and home. Faculty members serve in this sense as mentors, facilitating teacher candidates' learning experiences and helping to support classroom teachers. As a result, successes can be measured in terms of shared impact on children and families. Shifting relationships among universities and partners is a complex effort (Cochran-Smith, 2004), requiring a change in the ways universities and birth-to-three agencies collaborate. For example, EHS teachers who have traditionally hosted teacher candidates must now have a strong voice in conversations about how future teachers are prepared in order to develop and implement more collaborative models. It is only through involving teachers in these conversations that preparation programs will expand their focus to truly address children's needs within the context of family and community (Early & Winton, 2001)—particularly in the case of infants and toddlers, for whom adequate teacher education is lacking (AACTE, 2004). These conversations form the building blocks of trust, enabling everyone involved to identify areas of potential mutual benefit, as well as educating university faculty about local needs so preparation activities and professional development may be designed to help address them.

Early Head Start teachers who have traditionally hosted teacher candidates must now have a strong voice in conversations about how future teachers are prepared

The implementation and integration of blended and tiered practices are areas where collaboration of this kind may help universities and EHS teachers to support each other. For teachers, these practices often represent new ways of collaborating. They require the identification and development of new resources and the formation of supportive, sustainable collaborative teams. Figure 2 displays four steps involved in building relationships to support teacher education and professional development, expanding the teaching and embedding of blended practices, and striving toward the integration of tiered models into EHS programs. These are steps EHS staff and university faculty may consult as they consider how to best support their individual and shared goals of supporting teacher candidates and infants/toddlers.

Figure 2

Laying a Foundation for Collaborative Blended/Tiered Practices in Early Head Start

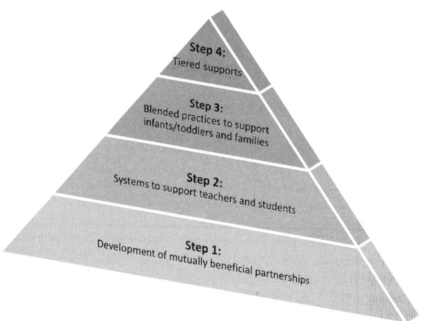

Step 4:
Tiered supports

Step 3:
Blended practices to support infants/toddlers and families

Step 2:
Systems to support teachers and students

Step 1:
Development of mutually beneficial partnerships

Step One: Developing a Partnership for Teacher Education and Professional Development

EHS is an example of a community-based agency offering a variety of child and family supports within an inclusive and family-centered program philosophy. EHS programs emphasize best practices for young children, including DEC's Recommended Practices (DEC, 2014) for Early Intervention (EI) and ECSE. These practices emphasize adaptations and modifications to early childhood environments in order to provide individualized supports for young children with special needs (Grisham-Brown et al., 2005). EHS teachers must possess essential knowledge, skills, and experiences with DAP for diverse infants and toddlers, including those with special needs (regardless of whether they receive EI services), particularly since EHS programs must provide opportunities for the enrollment of infants and toddlers with special needs and collaborate with professionals providing services under Part C of IDEA. These competencies support blending and can be both built and shared with teacher candidates within a model that positively impacts children and their families. Within a co-mentoring relationship alongside university faculty, EHS teachers may model these blended practices for teacher

Figure 3
Checklist of Strategies to Support Successful, Sustainable University-EHS Partnerships for Collaborative Teacher Education and Development

Partnership Principles	Considerations for University and EHS Partners
Commitment and trust in shared expertise (Kruger et al., 2009)	☐ Are EHS and university leaders committed to the partnership? ☐ Is ample time provided for relationship building? ☐ Do faculty and EHS staff have clearly defined roles and responsibilities? ☐ Are all stakeholders (teachers, teacher educators, teacher candidates, caregivers) recognized as contributors? ☐ Are there established, accessible methods of communication?
Mutual benefit in collaboration (Kruger et al., 2009)	☐ Are stakeholders collaborating to enhance classroom experiences and development of EHS children? ☐ Have stakeholders discussed their desired partnership outcomes? ☐ Do all stakeholders benefit from their contributions to the partnership? ☐ Are stakeholder experiences evaluated to determine the degree of mutual benefit?
Reciprocity in partnership roles (Kruger et al., 2009)	☐ Are stakeholders willing to learn from the knowledge, skills, and experiences of others? ☐ Do partnership meetings occur regularly? ☐ Are all stakeholders provided leadership opportunities? ☐ Do all stakeholders have a voice in partnership developments?
Value of field experiences for teacher preparation and professional development	☐ Does the partnership consistently prioritize children and families? ☐ Does the partnership enhance or expand EHS services for infants, toddlers, and families? ☐ Are all stakeholders welcomed as active classroom participants? ☐ Do university and EHS faculty collaborate to develop and support requirements of field experiences?
Mentorship as a professional responsibility	☐ Do stakeholders feel responsible for sharing their knowledge, skills, and experiences with others? ☐ Have stakeholders identified their knowledge, skills, and resources to support teacher candidates? ☐ Have stakeholders collaborated to define their mentoring roles? ☐ Are structural supports available (e.g. time, compensation, professional development, other resources)?

candidates while at the same time expanding their own skills in individualizing instruction through the consultative support of early childhood faculty.

EHS and teacher education programs considering entering into a partnership may use Figure 3 to identify their readiness for collaboration, structures that will support it, and strengths and areas of need. These principles are reflective of DEC's Code of Ethics (2009) regarding Professional Collaboration. Careful consideration and communication around these themes throughout the partnership will better ensure its responsiveness to the needs of everyone involved, as well as provide a foundation for collaborative teacher education.

To initiate a university-EHS partnership, university faculty meet with EHS administrators to identify the strengths and needs of the EHS center and its teachers. The EHS administrators may share their assessment of the teachers' interests and competencies in mentoring teacher candidates, but classroom teachers must be involved in the early conversations as well. EHS teachers indicate what knowledge and skills they may offer novice teacher candidates, as well as identify their own professional goals to be supported through university resources and professional development. Through these early discussions university faculty may identify EHS teacher mentors and topics in need of professional development. They might also identify other key members of the EHS community who can support the partnership—in particular, family support personnel, teacher leaders, and parents (or caregivers in instances where extended family or other adults fill the primary parenting role). Once interested EHS teachers commit to mentoring, the partnership may move on to identify the roles and responsibilities of each of these participants.

Step Two: Building Support Systems for Preservice and Practicing Teachers

Once EHS and university partners are cognizant of their roles and committed to partnering, EHS teachers may be better supported to mentor candidates to develop their emerging professional competencies, including: (1) DAP for infants and toddlers; (2) communication with families, who can be encouraged to share their experiences and introduce candidates to their young children; (3) identification of children's individual needs and appropriate interventions for school and home; and (4) implementation of assessments to monitor children's progress and responses to intervention. All of these competencies support blended practices (DEC, 2009; NAEYC, 2009). For EHS teachers to mentor teacher candidates without diminishing their focus on teaching, those candidates must engage as active members of the classroom community. Therefore they must not only be sufficiently prepared to begin their experiences in infant/toddler classrooms by establishing collegial relationships with teachers and serving as active participants, observers/assessors, and novice teachers, but also *supported consistently by*

For teachers to mentor teacher candidates without diminishing their focus on teaching, those candidates must be supported consistently by faculty as they bridge theory to practice.

faculty throughout their field-based experiences as they intentionally bridge theory to practice (Ball & Cohen, 1999). In TLLSC, for instance, teacher candidates are directly supervised on-site by university faculty from the beginning to the end of each field-based experience, which also includes learning activities outside the birth-to-three classroom and field trips to explore resources in the surrounding community.

Once initial needs are addressed and a support system is in place, faculty can implement an observation/evaluation system for candidates' interactions with children. Using a formal observation tool such as the Classroom Assessment Scoring System (CLASS; LaParo, Hamre, & Pianta, 2012) provides systematic data on candidates as they learn to facilitate both social-emotional and cognitive/language development using specific, observable DAPs. Classroom visits also offer a valuable opportunity for faculty to provide observational data on infants/toddlers to support EHS teachers; these data, in turn, can help facilitate the subsequent implementation of tiered supports in association with appropriate professional development.

Next, systems that support both teacher candidates and teachers themselves can be set in place. One way to address the goal of integrating teacher education and professional development is for university faculty to implement MTSS for the teacher candidates themselves, and to involve EHS teachers in these systems (Winton, 2013). MTSS or Response to Intervention (RTI) practices involve the use of data to identify children in need of interventions; interventions/supports increase in intensity and frequency in response to children's needs in any area of development. Teachers' practice may also improve through the use of multi-tiered supports in professional development (Myers, Simonsen, & Sugai, 2011; Winton, 2013). Universal, targeted, and intensive supports can be developed by faculty to address the needs of candidates in a particular EHS setting. This serves a parallel goal of providing a context for professional development with teachers on the use of tiered supports for young children. EHS teachers may then begin learning about tiered models for infants and toddlers having already collaborated in a similar way to support teacher candidates.

Universal Supports

Universal supports should be developed to promote candidates' learning of developmentally appropriate and blended practices. These supports should address and monitor the candidates' performance, including their interactions with children, families, and their EHS mentors. We will discuss some of these supports next.

Progress Monitoring Tool. Prior to candidates' involvement in classrooms, university faculty should consult with classroom teachers to select a shared method for assessing candidates' interactions with infants and toddlers. An evaluation tool such as the CLASS (LaParo et al., 2012) provides candidates with consistent, specific feedback relative to dimensions of DAP. The CLASS dimensions for effective teaching (which include Positive/Negative Climate, Teacher Sensitivity, Facilitation of Learning/Development, and Language Modeling/Support for infants/toddlers, as well as Teacher Sensitivity, Regard for Child Perspectives, Behavior Guidance, and Quality of Feedback for toddlers only) support EHS teachers in identifying specific aspects of their own practice that must be made explicit for candidates, thus supporting mentoring relationships while acting as a professional development and self-evaluation tool for EHS teachers. The CLASS dimensions also align neatly with DEC's Recommended Practices (DEC, 2014) regarding adult-child interaction and support for social-emotional competence. Feedback should be provided regularly (weekly at a minimum) to monitor candidate progress; in the case of the CLASS, feedback may take the form of numerical ratings depicted in line graphs to display growth (Figure 3) as well as narrative feedback on candidates' individual strengths and areas of need. EHS teachers must be involved in this evaluation process. Not only is their feedback essential, but this also provides an opportunity for them to build their awareness of evidence-based practices, which may in turn lead to the identification of future professional development topics.

Activity Plans. Candidates collaborate with each other, teachers, and faculty to design and implement both planned (see Table 1) and informal activities for each day spent in infant/toddler classrooms. These activities might also be designed with informal input from parents regarding their children's interests, experiences, and needs. Implemented activities teach candidates about features of developmentally appropriate learning environments and opportunities for learning through daily routines. They also provide additional intentionally designed experiences and increased engagement for children in EHS classrooms. After activities are implemented, candidates should reflect on them with their peers and mentors to make recommendations for improving their future practice, subsequently sharing them as an online resource (e.g., via a Google site accessible to all partners).

Teaching Videos. Provided consent is obtained from families, activities led by candidates may be video recorded and uploaded to a web-based platform such as *VoiceThread* (VoiceThread LLC, 2014). The videos provide candidates an opportunity for personal reflection and real-time

Table 1
Excerpt from a Teacher Candidate Activity Plan: Yay! Let's Play with Clay!

Steps in the activity	What will adults do and say to model, respond to, and encourage language?	What will you be expecting children to do during this stage?	Blended practice: What accommodations will be considered or needed?
1. Get children's attention, prepare for play by putting smocks on.	Draw children over to table, model squeezing and pounding of clay. Support children as they attempt to put smocks on. "We are going to have some fun with clay!" Include targeted verbal/physical support with smocks as needed	Pick up smocks, place arms in holes to whatever degree they can independently, and wait as smock is fastened.	Behavioral support: Use 'First, Then' chart with M to transition to table by putting smock on.
2. Allow the children to take/freely explore clay.	Supervise the children as they play with clay. "Clay!" "Roll!" "Pat!" "Push!" and adjectives to describe color/texture.	Look at clay and possibly pick up clay. Children explore the clay and all of the things it can do.	Initially, allow some children to explore the clay without direction of any kind. Work on K's IFSP Goal: Plays with a variety of toys and textures so that she may participate more actively in group activities.

Table 1 (*continued*)

Steps in the activity	What will adults do and say to model, respond to, and encourage language?	What will you be expecting children to do during this stage?	Blended practice: What accommodations will be considered or needed?
3. Model and support children's exploration.	Model placing the clay in front of us and how to spread and soften it. Adults will narrate and insert selected questions. Provide positive and descriptive feedback.	Manipulate clay and use tools to explore and alter clay forms, shapes, texture.	Encourage K to explore clay with both hands. Work on M's IFSP goal: Imitates simple actions (with verbal direction) and single words during play and daily routines; imitates peer's actions.
4. Wash hands when children indicate they are done.	Support children in the steps of hand washing. Ask targeted questions to get children to initiate steps, narrate routine.	Complete this routine with as much independence as possible.	Use 'First, Then' chart with M to transition from table to hand washing and then classroom centers. Work on K's IFSP goal: Change from one activity to the next without becoming upset.

peer feedback of their teaching. The videos serve as a progress monitoring tool for faculty and teachers, as well as a tool for identifying candidates' areas of strength or needed improvements.

Targeted Supports

For candidates who require additional input to make adequate progress, targeted supports can be developed. The examples described next are universal supports that may be increased in frequency/intensity or combined to serve as targeted supports.

For candidates new to interacting with infants and toddlers, explanations of DAP are not enough.

Additional Feedback. For candidates making limited progress, faculty and teachers should provide additional feedback that explicitly identifies areas of concern and provides specific recommendations for improvement. Feedback should be offered both through the chosen evaluation tool (e.g. CLASS; LaParo et al., 2012) as well as in person during classroom observations, so that candidates may receive *in-the-moment* encouragement and recommendations for improvement, enabling them to capitalize on their time interacting with infants and toddlers.

Modeling. For candidates new to interacting with infants and toddlers, explanations of DAP may not be enough. Faculty and teachers can model that practice with infants/toddlers, allowing candidates to see how adults support child development (including practices proving challenging to enact). Candidates are then supported in their understanding of teaching the youngest children, who in turn receive even more of the positive attention they crave. Modeling is also particularly important in teaching infants and toddlers with special needs. Role play of interactions with families can also be used similarly.

Faculty and teachers model practice with infants/toddlers, allowing candidates to see how adults support child development.

Guiding Self-Reflection. Video recorded activities may be shared among candidates, who can be directed to view specific portions of videos that highlight opportunities to implement DAP or challenges that warrant discussion. Faculty and teachers may also identify and share peer videos that exemplify effective teaching practices.

Figure 4
Graph of Preservice Teacher Progress on 5 CLASS Dimensions With Tier 2 Support Initiated in Week 2

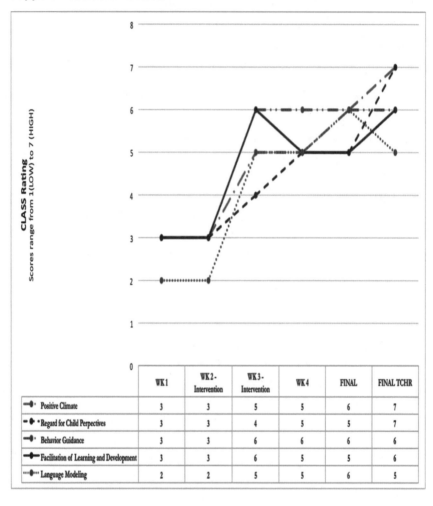

	WK1	WK2-Intervention	WK3-Intervention	WK4	FINAL	FINAL TCHR
Positive Climate	3	3	5	5	6	7
Regard for Child Perspectives	3	3	4	5	5	7
Behavior Guidance	3	3	6	6	6	6
Facilitation of Learning and Development	3	3	6	5	5	6
Language Modeling	2	2	5	5	6	5

Figure 4 displays CLASS (LaParo et al., 2012) data for a candidate who required individual support after two weeks in an EHS classroom with little progress. In this example, university faculty and EHS teachers provided targeted supports to the undergraduate candidate around several CLASS dimensions (LaParo et al., 2012). After a one-on-one meeting with university faculty to identify areas of need, the candidate was given additional feedback during classroom observations, modeling of best practice by university faculty and EHS teachers, and videos of exemplary activities led by her peers. University faculty shared the graph displayed in Figure 4 with the candidate and EHS teachers to identify the candidate's challenges and display her response to interventions. Figure 4 demonstrates the potential of intensive collaboration and individualized support for teacher candidates, as this candidate made immediate progress in response to these supports. Specifically, these supports laid the groundwork for the success of future professional development with EHS teachers by illustrating the importance of progress monitoring when transferring the use of tiered models from teacher education to practice with infants and toddlers.

Tiered supports laid the groundwork for the success of future professional development with EHS teachers by illustrating the importance of progress monitoring when transferring the use of tiered models from teacher education to practice

Intensive Supports

The occasional candidate may continue with minimal progress, even with universal and targeted supports in place. In these instances, faculty and teachers must collaborate to provide intensive interventions. Intensive supports can include expanded targeted supports, as well as additional strategies.

Individual Improvement Plan. Faculty and teachers may intervene with candidates experiencing acute difficulty in their interactions with infants/toddlers and/or families to develop individual improvement plans. Faculty, teachers, and candidates should develop specific goals and strategies for achieving the goals so candidates positively contribute to EHS classrooms; these goals must be monitored regularly and adapted as needed. Additional members of the EHS staff may provide support for these plans in order to address candidates' knowledge or skill gaps.

Conferencing. Holding individual meetings with candidates to discuss their EHS experiences can provide insight into their perceived strengths, areas of need, and a safe space to generate strategies that may increase their effectiveness in supporting children and families.

Step Three: Supporting Blended Practices in EHS Classrooms

Blending supports the development and full participation of all children and involves evidence-based practices from both ECE and ECSE

Figure 5
Questions for Teams to Consider When Collaborating to Enhance Blended Practices

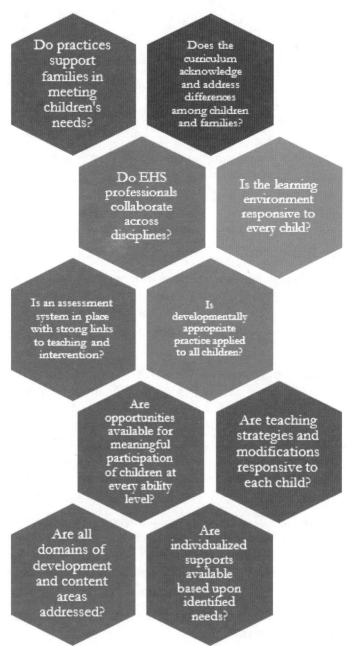

(Grisham-Brown et al., 2005). Blending requires us to continuously examine our work as educators to ensure that every child receives the benefit of DAP and inclusive practices, along with individualized strategies and services to meet their needs. Figure 5 presents key aspects of blended practice (Grisham-Brown & Pretti-Frontczak, 2011), phrased as reflective questions for practitioners to consider in relation to their own work; as teams plan to address these interrelated questions, they build structures that support blended practices. Teams (whether they consist of teachers, EHS staff, or all members of a university-EHS partnership) may reflect on these questions (which are not designed to follow a specific sequence) to identify strengths, resources, and areas to address as they work to enhance their blended practice.

These practices are driven by teachers, but they also include the collaborative framework that integrates and supports those skills. EHS program principles and practices (U.S. Department of Health and Human Services, 2014) are aligned extensively with the principles of inclusion and with DEC's Recommended Practices (DEC, 2014). EHS can support blended practices and, ideally, blended preparation. Teachers prepared through field-based teacher education programs that both include and support EHS programs can be provided with direct experience in making inclusive practices work through recognizing the importance of responding to each child's individual characteristics, strengths, and needs.

Figure 6
A Teacher Candidate Uses Universal Strategies to Support Toddler Learning and Development

Teacher candidates and teacher education faculty can join the list of EHS stakeholders responsible for supporting children and families (Kruger et al., 2009) and play a role in supporting blended practices in EHS. Candidates learn and implement blended practices by working with EHS teachers and faculty to assess the learning environment, examine the curriculum and identify ways to enhance it, develop targeted activities/interventions, and support classroom assessment procedures. EHS can provide a context within which they must also learn to implement these practices with culturally and linguistically diverse families. When EHS teachers share their experiences and expertise in learning and applying culturally responsive practices, they provide authentic contexts for candidates to examine, reflect upon, and begin to embody these practices themselves (Murrell, 2000). Encouraging candidates to dialogue with teachers and caregivers around children's lived experiences increases the cultural continuity between home and school and directly supports the implementation of individualized services and supports (Valdés, Bunch, Snow, Lee, & Matos, 2005).

Early Head Start provides a context within which candidates must learn to implement these blended practices with culturally and linguistically diverse families.

Activity Plans

In addition to all of the activities previously mentioned, activity plans provide an additional context where candidates directly apply their emerging knowledge and skills in blended practice. Activity plans such as the one displayed in Table 1 can include links to not only DAP, EHS and curriculum standards, and strategies for adult-child interaction, but also to individual instructional and assessment practices required for children with special needs. The clay activity in Table 1 was planned by undergraduate ECSE teacher candidates and includes examples of candidates considering the Individualized Family Service Plans goals of individual children, specific accommodations for toddlers with special needs, and additional language supports for children who might require them. Teachers supported candidates in implementing these strategies by sharing IFSP goals and facilitating conversation with visiting EI practitioners and families. Through these collaborations, candidates learned about the local, federal, and ethical guidelines related to serving infants and toddlers with disabilities and/ or developmental delays (DEC, 2014). They also learned from direct experience with collaborative models of service delivery (where teachers, EI practitioners, and caregivers work together to meet the needs of children with special needs), which are essential to the success of quality blended practices.

Teaching Videos and Faculty Support

Videos (and observations) of teacher candidates' planned activities and CLASS evaluations serve as tools to provide consistent feedback from teachers, faculty, and even peers. They are accepted and supported as novices in the field, but are still held accountable for providing high quality, individualized services for infants and toddlers in alignment with evidence-based practices for young children with disabilities (DEC, 2014). They are better able to accomplish this (and expand on their skills) with constant feedback before, during, and after their planned activities and interactions. EHS teachers share their expertise in linking classroom practices to the routines and needs of families in accordance with the principles of positive relationships and continuity, which are integrated into all EHS programs. Teachers and parents/caregivers can help candidates to draw connections between their program assignments (including planned activities) and children's home environments.

Figure 7
A Teacher Candidate Implements Targeted Supports During Hand Washing

Targeted Preparation on Blended Practices

Both teacher candidates and EHS teachers can benefit from consultation with faculty on their own blended practices. These interactions take place outside of the EHS classroom and serve as both professional preparation and professional development.

Step Four: Integrating Tiered Supports for Infants/Toddlers and Families

The collaboration of faculty, teachers, families, and candidates in EHS classrooms (and tiered supports to address candidates' needs) provides a context within which a more systematic approach to intervention and assessment (namely, RTI) may be considered. RTI frameworks are a means for implementing a hierarchy of support that is differentiated through a data-based decision-making process (Greenwood et al. 2011; National Professional Development Center on Inclusion [NPDCI], 2012). In early childhood settings, RTI supports must ideally include not only these components, but research-based strategies and practices as well. The use of tiered models with infants and toddlers is an emerging area of research, and limited information is available about the outcomes of RTI in birth to three (DEC, NAEYC, & NHSA, 2013). Furthermore, the implementation of RTI in EHS programs involves more than university faculty and teacher candidates; all EHS stakeholders have a role in this system, and the strategies presented here represent only one step in a long-term process that must be considered and undertaken carefully. However, field-based partnership models do hold great potential for building some of the knowledge, skills, and structures necessary for RTI to succeed.

In a partnership model, EHS teachers increase the transparency of their teaching so candidates may examine and embody the skills of an effective infant/toddler teacher during their initial field experiences. These skills include identifying children who may benefit from targeted interventions (regardless of whether an RTI framework is in use). EHS teachers can also facilitate communication between candidates and parents/caregivers and work with faculty to develop intensive interventions addressing specific needs of children at home and in the center. University faculty must coordinate, oversee, and evaluate candidates' development of interventions, providing continual guidance to ensure their appropriateness and participate directly in their delivery. Through these experiences, EHS teachers are introduced to elements of tiered models that are difficult to develop, implement, and maintain without additional assistance.

Both teachers and teacher candidates can be formally introduced to specific tiered models, including the ECE RTI Framework developed by DEC, NAEYC, and NHSA (2013), which emphasizes universal, targeted, and intensive supports in a structure that is aligned with the principles of DAP and applicable to all domains of infant/toddler development. The Pyramid Model (Fox, Carta, Strain, Dunlap, & Hemmeter, 2010) is another approach to the planning and delivery of tiered supports that is inclusive of infant/toddler settings. The Pyramid Model specifically addresses social-emotional development, and teachers may find its tiers to be somewhat familiar (universal supports, for instance, consist of Nurturing and Responsive Relationships and High Quality Supportive Environments - see Figure 6), based upon their own experiences with DAP, as well as having worked directly and explicitly with candidates on understanding and embodying these practices in the classroom (and providing feedback via CLASS, LaParo et al., 2012). As tiered models are introduced, experiences within the partnership can be referenced in both teacher education seminars and professional development for EHS teachers.

In the classroom, EHS teachers may recommend activities to teacher candidates because they have specific concerns about a child and are seeking ways to address that concern in a developmentally appropriate and engaging way - see Figure 7. In this sense, activity plans (particularly when repeated over a series of days) developed to enhance the universal curriculum, become targeted interventions that address not only social-emotional skills but *all* developmental domains, thus serving the EHS priority of recognizing and preventatively addressing individual needs.

EHS teachers, candidates, and university faculty ideally include parents/caregivers in this partnership so that they may share their knowledge and experiences. This involvement is essential to developing seamless continuums of support as children move on to other early childhood pro-

Parental/caregiver involvement is essential to developing seamless continuums of support for infants and toddlers

grams and, eventually, into elementary school. Caregivers provide the essential link to children's home environments (including language, culture, routines, and priorities), enabling candidates and teachers to adapt their classroom practices to better match caregiver values and provide an increased continuity of care (Hunter & Hemmeter, 2009). Even in the absence of a formal tiered model, these teams can identify areas of need across developmental domains and design/monitor individualized interventions to implement in the classroom and/or at home (Hunter &

Hemmeter, 2009). Candidates then help to record the child's response to the intervention at home and school, working with all partners to adapt the interventions as needed.

Wherever interventions are implemented, faculty must also ensure that a framework for the evaluation of intervention fidelity has been put in place. When interventions are implemented with integrity, children respond positively and exhibit improved outcomes (Collier-Meek, Fallon, Sanetti, & Maggin, 2013). Faculty guide candidates in selecting and developing targeted and intensive interventions, providing specific performance feedback on implemented interventions. This supports candidates' competency in implementation with fidelity, improving teaching effectiveness as a result (Hagermoser-Sanetti, Fallon, & Collier-Meek, 2013). Likewise, this also serves to enhance EHS teachers' attentiveness to consistent implementation of interventions, since they themselves may struggle to consistently implement interventions in context. In TLLSC, candidates continue their preparation around these practices as they transition to other early childhood settings in later sequences.

A partnership model plays a beneficial role in first planting the seeds of tiered supports, with subsequent program-wide professional development to expand the range of supports and services available to EHS families. As a result, EHS team members are better prepared to contextualize (and, later, apply) these practices with continued faculty support. Meanwhile, candidates learn from these initial teacher education experiences that they can collaborate successfully to design, implement, and monitor interventions with fidelity while simultaneously addressing the universal needs of the whole class through daily interactions and planned activities. This balancing of teacher roles is a high-level teaching skill that candidates often do not get an opportunity to practice until they reach their culminating student teaching experiences.

Summary

Blended practices and tiered models present complex challenges when applied to infant/toddler settings such as EHS. As early childhood teacher education is increasingly re-envisioned as an equal partnership among university faculty/candidates, EHS teachers, and infants/toddlers and their families, gaps between the preparation of teachers and their experiences in the field will be narrowed. Strong links between preparation and practice are essential to the success of blended practices and tiered models, as these collaborative approaches are most effectively mastered when teacher education and professional development are both embedded in contexts where we serve children and families. By supporting each member of these partnerships in meaningful roles related to the professional development of both preservice and practicing teachers, university and EHS partners can play a direct role in the collaborative relationships necessary to build, implement, and sustain blended and tiered practices with the youngest children.

Note

For more information, please contact Adam S. Kennedy at Akenne5@luc.edu

The authors express their gratitude to Cathy Rokusek and the teachers and staff of the Easter Seals Near South Side Child Development Center for their contributions to this partnership and for their dedication to high quality services for all young children. This work was supported in part by the U.S. Department of Education, Office of Special Education Programs (OSEP) under a grant in Personnel Preparation in EI/ECSE (#H325K120172).

References

American Association of Colleges for Teacher Education. (2004). *The early childhood challenge: Preparing high-quality teachers for a changing society* [White paper]. Washington, DC: Author. Retrieved June 25, 2014, from http://aacte.org/pdf/Programs/Early_Childhood/ECEpaper.pdf

American Association of Colleges of Teacher Education. (2010). *21st century knowledge and skills in educator preparation* [White paper]. Washington, DC: Author. Retrieved from June 25, 2014, from http://aacte.org/pdf/Publications/Reports_Studies/AACTE-P21%20White%20Paper%20vFINAL.pdf

Ball, D. & Cohen, D. (1999). Developing practice, developing practitioners: Toward a practice-based theory of professional education. In L. Darling-Hammond & G. Sykes (Eds.), *Teaching as the learning profession* (pp. 3-32). San Francisco: Jossey-Bass.

Cochran-Smith, M. (2004). The problem of teacher education. *Journal of Teacher Education, 55*(4), 295-299.

Collier-Meek, M. A., Fallon, L. M., Sanetti, L. M., & Maggin, D. M. (2013). Focus on implementation: Assessing and promoting treatment fidelity. *Teaching Exceptional Children, 45*(5), 52-59.

Darling-Hammond, L. (Ed.). (1994). *Professional development schools: Schools for developing a profession* (Vol. 1234). New York: Teachers College Press.

Darling-Hammond, L. & Baratz-Snowden, J. (Eds.). (2007). A good teacher in every classroom: Preparing the highly qualified teachers our children deserve. *Educational Horizons, 85*(2), 111-132.

Division for Early Childhood. (2009). *Code of ethics of the Division for Early Childhood (DEC) of the Council for Exceptional Children.* Retrieved June 25, 2014, from http://dec.membershipsoftware.org/files/Position%20Statement%20and%20Papers/Member%20Code%20of%20Ethics.pdf

Division for Early Childhood. (2014). *DEC recommended practices in early intervention/early childhood special education.* Retrieved June 25, 2014, from http://dec.membershipsoftware.org/files/DEC_RPs_%205-1-14.pdf

Division for Early Childhood, National Association for the Education of Young Children, & National Head Start Association, [DEC/NAEYC/NHSA]. (2013). *Frameworks for Response to Intervention in early childhood: Description and implications.* Missoula, MT: Author.

Early, D. M. & Winton, P. J. (2001). Preparing the workforce: Early childhood teacher preparation at 2- and 4-year institutions of higher education. *Early Childhood Research Quarterly, 16*(3), 285-306.

Fox, L., Carta, J. J., Strain, P. S., Dunlap, G., & Hemmeter, M. L. (2010). Response to intervention and the Pyramid Model. *Infants & Young Children, 23*(1), 3-13.

Greenwood, C. R., Bradfield, T., Kaminski, R., Linas, M., Carta, J. J., & Nylander, D. (2011). The response to intervention (RTI) approach in early childhood. *Focus on Exceptional Children, 43*(9), 1-22.

Grisham-Brown, J., Hemmeter, M. L., & Pretti-Frontczak, K. (2005). *Blended practices for teaching young children in inclusive settings.* Baltimore: Paul H. Brookes.

Grisham-Brown, J. & Pretti-Frontczak, K. (2011). *Assessing young children in inclusive settings: The blended practice approach.* Baltimore: Paul H. Brookes.

Hagermoser-Sanetti, L. M., Fallon, L. M., & Collier Meek, M. A. (2013). Increasing teacher treatment integrity through performance feedback provided by school personnel. *Psychology in the Schools, 50*(2), 134-150.

Hunter, A. & Hemmeter, M. L. (2009). The center on the social and emotional foundations for early learning: Addressing challenging behavior in infants and toddlers. *Zero to Three, 29*(3), 5-12.

Kennedy, A. & Heineke, A. (2014). Re-envisioning the role of universities in early childhood teacher preparation: Partnerships for 21st century learning. *Journal of Early Childhood Teacher Education, 35*(3), 1-17.

Kruger, T., & Teaching Australia - Australian Institute for Teaching and School Leadership. (2009). *Effective and sustainable university-school partnerships: Beyond determined efforts by inspired individuals.* Acton, A.C.T: Teaching Australia, Australian National University.

LaParo, K., Hamre, B., & Pianta, R. (2012). *Classroom assessment scoring system (CLASS) manual, toddler.* Baltimore: Paul H. Brookes.

Lim, C. I. & Able-Boone, H. (2005). Diversity competencies within early childhood teacher preparation: Innovative practices and future directions. *Journal of Early Childhood Teacher Education, 26*(3), 225-238.

McDonald, M., Tyson, K., Brayko, K., Bowman, M., Delport, J., & Shimomura, F. (2011). Innovation and impact in teacher education: Community-based organizations as field placements for preservice teachers. *Teachers College Record, 113*(8), 1668-1700.

Murrell, P. C., Jr. (2000). Community teachers: A conceptual framework for preparing exemplary urban teachers. *Journal of Negro Education, 69*(4), 338-348.

Myers, D. M., Simonsen, B., & Sugai, G. (2011). Increasing teachers' use of praise with a response-to-intervention approach. *Education & Treatment of Children, 34*(1), 35-59.

National Association for the Education of Young Children. (2009). *Where we stand on professional preparation standards: A position statement*. Washington, DC: Author. Retrieved June 25, 2014, from http://www.naeyc.org/files/naeyc/file/positions/programStandards.pdf

National Council for Accreditation of Teacher Education. (2011). *Transforming teacher education through clinical practice: A national strategy to prepare effective teachers*. Washington, DC: Author. Retrieved June 25, 2014, from http://www.ncate.org/LinkClick.aspx?fileticket=zzeiB1OoqPk%3D&tabid=715

National Professional Development Center on Inclusion. (2012). *Response to intervention (RTI) in early childhood: Building consensus on the defining features*. Chapel Hill: University of North Carolina, FPG Child Development Institute. Retrieved June 25, 2014, from http://npdci.fpg.unc.edu/sites/npdci.fpg.unc.edu/files/resources/NPDCI-RTI-Concept-Paper-FINAL-2-2012.pdf

Rust, F. (2010). Shaping new models for teacher education. *Teacher Education Quarterly, 37*(2), 5-18.

U.S. Department of Health and Human Services. (2014). *About Early Head Start*. Retrieved June 25, 2014, from http://eclkc.ohs.acf.hhs.gov/hslc/tta-system/ehsnrc/Early%20Head%20Start/about.html

Valdés, G., Bunch, G., Snow, C., Lee, C., & Matos, L. (2005). Enhancing the development of students' language(s). In L. Darling-Hammond & J. Bransford (Eds.), *Preparing teachers for a changing world: What teachers should learn and be able to do* (pp. 126-168). San Fransisco: Jossey-Bass

VoiceThread LLC. (2014). *Voice Thread*. Available from http://voicethread.com/

Winton, P. (2013). Professional development: Supporting the evidence-based early childhood practitioner. In V. Buysse & E. Peisner-Feinberg (Eds.), *Handbook of response to intervention in early childhood* (pp. 325-338). Baltimore: Brookes.

Moving
Forward
Resources for Supporting Blended Practices

Ashley Lyons ME.d.
Kent State University

Throughout Monograph No. 16, the authors referenced or recommended a number of resources that may assist providers, practitioners, administrators, families, and other stakeholders with the implementation of blended practices. From each article in this issue, we have selected specific resources that would be of particular value to our readers and have provided a brief description of how the resource can support blending practices. In particular, the resources we have selected have the potential to support both individual stakeholders and programs in the identification and implementation of the foundational components of inclusive early childhood environments that will lead to the use of blended practices that are appropriate to meet the needs of the children and families they serve.

Resource: Sandall, S. R., & Schwartz, I. S. (2008). *Building blocks for teaching preschoolers with special needs* (2nd ed.). Baltimore: Brookes.

Referenced or recommended in: "Blending Practices to Support Inclusion: A Process to Guide Itinerant ECSE Services" (Laurie A. Dinnebeil and William F. McInerney); "Quality Instruction Through Complete Learning Trials: Blending Intentional Teaching With Embedded Instruction" (Erin E. Barton, Crystal Crowe Bishop, and Patricia Snyder); "Adapting Lesson Plans for Preschoolers: Addressing

State Early Learning Standards" (Emily Dorsey, Natalie Danner, and Bernadette Laumann); and "Together Is Better: Environmental Teaching Practices to Support All Children's Learning" (Philippa H. Campbell and Suzanne A. Milbourne)

How this can support blending instruction: *"Updated for today's educators—especially those new to inclusion—the second edition of this best-selling guide is the lifeline preschool teachers need to fully include children with disabilities in their classrooms. Easy to use with any existing curriculum, including Creative Curriculum and HighScope,* Building Blocks *gives educators three types of practical, research-based inclusion strategies that promote progress in critical areas like behavior, emergent literacy, and peer relationships"* (description from Brookes Publishing). This resource includes a wide variety of planning templates that can be used to support blending practices in the inclusive classroom. For example, the ELO-at-a-Glance template supports professionals (and even parents) in planning for a learning exchange by identifying the learning objective, the routines that will be targeted, the actions the adult will take, the statements and feedback the adult will provide to the child, the materials that will be needed (if any), and the number of planned opportunities to address the learning objective.

Available for purchase at: http://products.brookespublishing.com/Building-Blocks-for-Teaching-Preschoolers-with-Special-Needs-Second-Edition-P223.aspx

Resource: Ohio Center for Autism and Low Incidence. (n.d.). *Autism Internet Modules* [AIM].

Referenced or recommended in: "Blending Practices to Support Inclusion: A Process to Guide Itinerant ECSE Services" (Laurie A. Dinnebeil and William F. McInerney)

How this can support blending instruction: Although the modules are designed to support instructional techniques for use with children autism spectrum disorders (ASDs), these modules can serve double-duty in two critical ways: (1) the strategies covered are useful for a wide range of children with varied learning needs beyond those with ASDs and, as such, can support instructional planning and blending practices in inclusive classrooms; and (2) the modules are comprehensive and encompass many instructional strategies, offering professionals who are partnering with those in the fields of early intervention/early childhood special education in-depth learning opportunities to ensure practices are implemented with fidelity. To access these free modules, simply create a free account. If you would like credit for participating in these modules, peruse the website to learn more about options and opportunities.

Available for free at: www.ocali.org (or http://www.autisminternetmodules.org/)

Resource: Epstein, A. S. (2014). *The intentional teacher: Choosing the best strategies for young children's learning* (2nd ed.). Washington, DC: National Association for the Education of Young Children.

Referenced or recommended in: "Quality Instruction Through Complete Learning Trials: Blending Intentional Teaching With Embedded Instruction" (Erin E. Barton, Crystal Crowe Bishop, and Patricia Snyder); and "Together Is Better: Environmental Teaching Practices to Support All Children's Learning" (Philippa H. Campbell and Suzanne A. Milbourne)

How this can support blending instruction: *Intentional instruction* refers to planning for instruction and embedding learning opportunities with thoughtful and careful attention paid to designing instruction to meet the unique needs of a variety of children. This resource provides support for determining which instructional strategies are best for different types of learners with diverse learning goals and offers specific strategies and ideas for use across developmental domains. For example, throughout the book examples are provided of what adult- vs. child-guided strategies might look like for specific learning objectives, with nonexamples included to make explicit how to best support children.

Available for purchase at: http://www.naeyc.org/store/node/553

Resource: Division for Early Childhood/National Association for the Education of Young Children (DEC/NAEYC). (2009, April). *Early childhood inclusion: A joint position statement of the Division for Early Childhood (DEC) and the National Association for the Education of Young Children (NAEYC).* Chapel Hill: The University of North Carolina, FPG Child Development Institute.

Referenced or recommended in: "Blending Practices to Support Inclusion: A Process to Guide Itinerant ECSE Services" (Laurie A. Dinnebeil and William F. McInerney); "Adapting Lesson Plans for Preschoolers: Addressing State Early Learning Standards" (Emily Dorsey, Natalie Danner, and Bernadette Laumann); "Together is Better: Environmental Teaching

Practices to Support All Children's Learning" (Philippa H. Campbell and Suzanne A. Milbourne); and "From All to Each and Every: Preparing Professionals to Support Children of Diverse Abilities" (Camille Catlett, Susan P. Maude, Melanie Nollsch, and Susan Simon)

How this can support blending instruction: This document describes the foundational components required for building effective inclusive environments. *"This joint position statement describes three defining features of inclusion: (1) children's access to a wide range of learning opportunities and environments, (2) children's participation in classroom routines and activities through scaffold learning, and (3) the provision of system-level supports such as professional development, opportunities for collaboration, and sufficient funding. . . .* [This resource] *provides direction and guidance for the design of programs blending best practices in early childhood education for all children with best practices in specialized instruction for children with disabilities"* (Dorsey, Danner, & Laumann, p. 44). Beyond helping professionals, families, and other stakeholders in becoming familiar with best practices in inclusion, this document could be used by professionals to discuss the joint statement in the context of data collected for accountability or how the statement aligns with a program's current vision, mission, and operating features.

Available for free at: http://www.dec-sped.org/papers

Resource: Grisham-Brown, J., Hemmeter, M. L., & Pretti-Frontczak, K. (2005). *Blended practices for teaching young children in inclusive settings*. Baltimore: Brookes.

Referenced or recommended in: "Quality Instruction Through Complete Learning Trials: Blending Intentional Teaching With Embedded Instruction" (Erin E. Barton, Crystal Crowe Bishop, and Patricia Snyder); "Adapting Lesson Plans for Preschoolers: Addressing State Early Learning Standards" (Emily Dorsey, Natalie Danner, and Bernadette Laumann); and "Infant/Toddler Professional Preparation and Development Using Blended Practices and Tiered Supports" (Adam S. Kennedy and Anna T. Lees)

How this can support blending instruction: Through the use of a curriculum framework approach (ASAP: assessment; scope and sequence; activities and instruction; and progress monitoring), this seminal resource offers educators a comprehensive guide to blending effective practices to meet the needs of all learners. This text is supported throughout by visual aids and vignettes that offer concrete examples of how each element of the curriculum framework can be implemented by blending practices.

The Curriculum-Based Assessment (CBA) rubric is an example of a particularly useful tool that supports professionals in evaluating a variety of CBAs for use with children with varied learning needs.

Available for purchase at: http://products.brookespublishing.com/Blended-Practices-for-Teaching-Young-Children-in-Inclusive-Settings-P545.aspx

Resource: Division of Early Childhood (DEC). (2007). *Promoting positive outcomes for children with disabilities: Recommendations for curriculum, assessment, and program evaluation.* Missoula, MT: Author.

Referenced or recommended in: "Blending Practices to Support Inclusion: A Process to Guide Itinerant ECSE Services" (Laurie A. Dinnebeil and William F. McInerney)

How this can support blending instruction: This document was written to serve as a companion to the 2003 joint position of the National Association for the Education of Young Children (NAEYC) and the National Association of Early Childhood Specialists in State Departments of Education (NAECS/SDE) on building effective early childhood systems for children birth to eight; it describes the position of DEC on meeting the needs of all young children, including those with exceptionalities. This position paper describes how professionals can use a curriculum framework and universal design for learning approach to support the learning of young children in blended classrooms. In addition to providing a broad framework for blending instruction to all interested stakeholders, this resource may be particularly useful to programs considering the development and/or refinement of professional development and program evaluation plans to support the program's effectiveness at blending instruction to meet the needs of all learners. Although the document is a position statement and thus there are no planning templates, it is a straightforward read that includes a number of visuals to demonstrate the big ideas programs should consider and offers a number of additional resources that can be consulted.

Available for free at: http://dec.membershipsoftware.org/files/Position%20Statement%20and%20Papers/Prmtg_Pos_Outcomes_Companion_Paper.pdf

Resource: Division for Early Childhood, National Association for the Education of Young Children, & National Head Start Association, [DEC/NAEYC/NHSA]. (2013). *Frameworks for Response to Intervention in early childhood: Description and implications.* Missoula, MT: Author.

Referenced or recommended in: "Infant/Toddler Professional Preparation and Development Using Blended Practices and Tiered Supports" (Adam S. Kennedy and Anna T. Lees);

How this can support blending instruction: This document describes how response to intervention (RtI) can be adapted for use in early childhood contexts. Whereas RtI has been used with school-aged children for more than 10 years to ensure that instruction is effective, tiered models of learning have more recently begun to take hold in programs serving younger children. Tiered models of learning are an important concept for contemporary blended classrooms and programs because their careful use can support universal design for learning (a practice that provides multiple means of representation, expression, and engagement for all children) and differentiation of instruction or support (through embedded learning opportunities and supports at higher tiers). As programs serving young children become increasingly inclusive in nature, the effective use of blended practices with fidelity will continue to be an important goal of professional development. This resource may serve as a starting point for conversations within programs to examine a) the extent to which complimentary practices are in place, b) and next steps to revise or adapt existing program guidelines to embrace a tiered model of learning that supports the use of blended practices and optimizes outcomes for all children.

Available for free at: http://www.dec-sped.org/papers

Resource: Winton, P., Buysse, V., Rous, B., Epstein, D., & Pierce, P. (2011). *CONNECT Module 5: Assistive Technology Interventions* [Web-based professional development curriculum]. Chapel Hill: The University of North Carolina, FPG Child Development Institute, CONNECT: The Center to Mobilize Early Childhood Knowledge.

Referenced or recommended in: "Together Is Better: Environmental Teaching Practices to Support All Children's Learning" (Philippa H. Campbell and Suzanne A. Milbourne)

How this can support blending instruction: The CONNECT Modules are a series of structured online learning activities that support professionals in practicing their application of specific skill sets that are important to their work in inclusive early childhood contexts by using a 5-step decision-making process. *Module 5: Assistive Technology Interventions* begins with a video overview of inclusion for children birth to five and offers several carefully selected resources to support this basic introduction. From there, learners are provided with a case example supported by video excerpts of a child in an inclusive classroom who is in need of assistive technology. In the scenario, learners are provided with the perspectives of both the teacher (who has not used assistive technology before) and the family (who is concerned about having their child in a classroom where the teacher does not have experience with important assistive technology). The module walks learners through the decision-making process to find a solution to make both the teacher and family confident in moving forward with the child being placed in the classroom. Other modules offered by CONNECT include Embedded Interventions; Transition; Communication for Collaboration; Family-Professional Partnerships; Dialogic Reading Practices; and Tiered Instruction. Each module offers extensive supports including activities, handouts, readings, videos, and additional resources. Individuals and programs will likely find these modules extremely useful for considering these important aspects of inclusion and blended practices as well as for supporting their own problem-solving skills and practices within their programs.

Available for free at: http://community.fpg.unc.edu/connect-modules/learners/module-5

For more information, contact Ashley Lyons at anlyons@kent.edu

YEC Monograph #16: Blended Practices
Editorial Team

Editors
Kristie Pretti-Frontczac, *B2K Solutions, Ltd.*
Jennifer Grisham-Brown, *University of Kentucky*
Lynn Sullivan, *Independent Consultant, Texas*

Moving Forward Columnist
Ashley Lyons, *Kent State University*

Managing Editors
Rosa Milagros Santos, *University of Illinois*
Mary Gravil, *University of Kentucky*

Reviewers
Serra Acar, *DEC Oregon Board Member*
Jay Buzhardt, *The University of Kansas*
Jennifer Champagne, *Oakland Schools, MI*
Ruby Chan, *University of Kansas*
Dana Childress, *Partnership for People with Disabilities at Virginia Commonwealth University*
Michelle Gatmaitan, *Kent State University*
Jennifer Grisham-Brown, *University of Kentucky*
Forrest Hancock, *Early Childhood Consultant*
Sarah Hawkins-Lear, *Morehead State University*
Sonja Hollan, *Region 4 Education Service Center*
Sanna Harjusola-Webb, *Kent State University*
Talina Jones, *NYC EICC Chair & Early Intervention Family Alliance*
Ruth Kaminski, *Dynamic Measurement Group*
Trudy Little, *Region 14 Education Service Center*
Eileen McCann, *Ridgewood Public Schools*
Tracy McElhattan, *The University of Kansas*
Kathleen McKinnon, *Penn State University*
Lydia Moore, *Kent State University*
Carla Peterson, *Iowa State University*
Diane Plunkett, *Fort Hays State University*
Megan Purcell, *Purdue University*
Jenna Weglarz-Ward, *University of Illinois*
Connie Wong, *Frank Porter Graham Child Development Institute at the University of North Carolina at Chapel Hill*
Suzanne Yockelson, *Brandman University*